# Bible Study
## TOGETHER

*Presented to:*

_____

_____

_____

*Presented by:*

_____

Published by: CreateSpace Independent Publishing Platform

Print Edition: 1.0
ISBN: 1985164639
ISBN-13: 978-1985164635

Printed in the United States of America, Feb 2018

# How To Use Our Study Journal
*A basic guide to having a quality quiet time with God.*

## Introduction

Christianity isn't about church attendance or charitable service. It's about being impacted by the love of God so that we come to share in His character and thereby make known His greatness. However, since people struggle to truly experience the love of God, they often try to live the Christian life without having the power to do so. This results in dead church attendance, attempts to settle a guilty conscience, or trying to fill emptiness by doing good to others. God never intended for us to live without His power moving us to obey Him and this is why we have created our study journal.

Our study journal is a guide to help you connect with God each day so that you can get charged to go out into the world and live the life you have been called to in Jesus. We have harnessed what many believers have learned over centuries and compiled it into our journal. Each day our journal will guide you to God's throne of grace where you can receive the wisdom and strength that produces the reflection of God's nature in you.

## Pursuit

In James 4:7-8 we are instructed on how to approach God's throne: "Submit yourselves therefore to God. Resist the devil, and he will flee from you. Draw near to God, and He will draw near to you..." James explains that we must yield our hearts to God and turn away from the lies of the Devil. Then we are to pursue God and He will

come to meet with us. Jeremiah prophesies about the type of pursuit God desires from us when God speaks through him saying, "And you shall seek me, and find me, when you shall search for me with all your heart" (Jeremiah 29:13). There is no better place to whole-heartedly search for God than in every word of the Bible. Our study journal will guide your pursuit of God through the whole Bible over the course of two years and each day God will come to reveal what He is speaking to you through its words.

## Pondering

Paul tells us, "Finally, brothers, whatever is true, whatever is honorable, whatever is just, whatever is pure, whatever is lovely, whatever is commendable, if there is any excellence, if there is anything worthy of praise, think about these things" (Philippians 4:8). Nothing fits this description more than the words of the Bible. Thinking and meditating on truth from the Bible brings our perspective of the world in line with the way God sees it. "Do not be conformed to this world, but be transformed by the renewal of your mind, that by testing you may discern what is the will of God, what is good and acceptable and perfect" (Romans 12:2). When we change our minds and start thinking like God, we begin to respond to the world the same way as Him. Each day our study journal will provide you with open-ended questions that will cause you to think about what God is speaking to you. As you ponder what God is teaching you, our journal helps you to solidify what you are learning by giving you space to write it down.

# Prayer

Jesus tells us, "Ask, and it will be given to you; seek, and you will find; knock, and it will be opened to you. For everyone who asks receives, and the one who seeks finds, and to the one who knocks it will be opened" (Matthew 7:7-8). Each day we encourage you to pray about what is going on in your life and the things you are reading in the Bible. James tells us, "If any of you lacks wisdom, let him ask God, who gives generously to all without reproach, and it will be given him" (James 1:5). Prayer is a two way conversation with God and Paul encourages us to pay attention while we pray (Colossians 4:2). As you immerse yourself in the Bible, God will bring back its words to answer the questions you ask Him (John 15:7). Each day we encourage you to write down notes about your time in prayer so you can see God's faithfulness as you ask and receive from Him.

# Practice

All too often people want Jesus to follow them and ask God to be with them while they build their own kingdom. However, God is calling each of us to "deny ourselves, take up our cross, and follow Him" (Luke 9:23). As you learn the heart of God by reading, meditating, and praying you will begin to see what God is doing around you personally and in your community. Our journal encourages you to consider what God is already doing and write down how you plan to join in and follow Him.

# Honor and Thanksgiving

No discussion about walking with God can be complete without pointing out the need to honor Him and give Him thanks. Paul teaches us, "For although they knew God, they did not honor Him as God or give thanks to Him, but they became futile in their thinking, and their foolish hearts were darkened" (Romans 1:21). Nothing will blind our eyes to the truth and shut up the heavens faster than neglecting these two things. Honoring God as God means we recognize His position and respond to it appropriately. Thankfulness toward God is the union of humility and faith. To be thankful, we must often humbly acknowledge that what we want is not the best that God has for us. We must yield in faith, trusting that God knows what is best. In this place of confidence in Him, we can "give thanks in every circumstance" (Ephesians 5:20). Without approaching God in honor and thanksgiving, any attempt to pursue God will be a hopeless endeavor.

# Conclusion

If you only read the Bible, its impact on your life will likely be minimal. In fact, you will probably get busy with other things and eventually stop. Nevertheless, if you take the time to consider the Bible's words and pray about what God is teaching you, your life will be radically altered forever. Using our study journal will help you digest the word of God and from it receive the sustaining life that will empower you to reflect the nature of God to a dark world. We encourage you to do this study with at least one other person. Please take some time and invite people to join your journey through the Bible.

## Daily Reading:

Genesis 1:1-2:4

## Study Journal Question:

1. What is the image of God, and what does it mean to be created in His image?
2. How does Genesis explaining that God created plants before He created the sun affect your understanding of creation?
3. How does the knowledge that God created both men and women in His image impact your perspective of the opposite sex?
4. In what ways did God call us to rest today?
5. How is God revealed in today's reading, and what does this mean for your life?

## Answers, Ponderings, and New Discoveries:

_____

_____

_____

_____

_____

_____

_____

_____

_____

_____

**Prayer Requests / Answers :** _____

_____

_____

_____

## What is God doing around you, and how can you join Him?

_____

_____

_____

## Together Challenge:

Find someone today to tell what you admire most about God's creation.

## Daily Reading:

Proverbs 8:1-36

## Study Journal Question:

1. In what ways does the Proverbs 8 description of wisdom differ from our culture's definition of wisdom?
2. How is God's wisdom expressed in creation?
3. What areas of your life do you lack wisdom, and how will you get this wisdom?
4. How did wisdom exist before everything was made?
5. How is God revealed in today's reading, and what does this mean for your life?

## Answers, Ponderings, and New Discoveries:

_____
_____
_____
_____
_____
_____
_____
_____
_____
_____
_____

**Prayer Requests / Answers :** _____
_____
_____
_____

## What is God doing around you, and how can you join Him?

_____
_____
_____

## Together Challenge:

Start a conversation with someone about Proverbs 8's description of wisdom.

## Daily Reading:

Proverbs 20:1-30, 1 John 1:1-2:6

## Study Journal Question:

1. Proverbs 20:9 asks, "Who can say, 'I have made my heart pure; I am clean from sin?'" How would you respond to this question in light of what John wrote?
2. How has God's love been perfected in your heart recently?
3. According to 1 John, how do Christians have fellowship with each other, and what does it look like?
4. How is God revealed in today's reading, and what does this mean for your life?

## Answers, Ponderings, and New Discoveries:

_____
_____
_____
_____
_____
_____
_____
_____
_____
_____
_____
_____

**Prayer Requests / Answers :** _____

_____
_____
_____

**What is God doing around you, and how can you join Him?**

_____
_____
_____

## Together Challenge:

Testify to someone about your own experience with God.

## Daily Reading:

Genesis 2:5-25, Proverbs 4:14-27, 1 John 2:7-29

## Study Journal Question:

1. Paul writes in Ephesians 5 that the two becoming one flesh is a symbol of Christ and the Church. How is the marriage of a man and woman similar to Christ and the Church?
2. Why do Proverbs and 1 John associate righteousness with light and darkness with wickedness?
3. What are some attributes of being in the light and of being in the darkness?
4. In what ways do you live in the light or the dark?
5. How is God revealed in today's reading, and what does this mean for your life?

## Answers, Ponderings, and New Discoveries:

_____
_____
_____
_____
_____
_____
_____
_____
_____
_____
_____

**Prayer Requests / Answers :** _____
_____
_____
_____

## What is God doing around you, and how can you join Him?

_____
_____
_____

## Together Challenge:

Ask the people in your life if there is anything you do to cause them to stumble.

## Daily Reading:

Genesis 3:1-24, 1 John 3:1-10

## Study Journal Question:

1. What excuses do you make for your shortcomings?
2. What are the characteristics of a child of God as described in 1 John 3?
3. What are the characteristics of a child of Devil as described in 1 John 3?
4. Why can't a child of God keep sinning, and how does he or she stop?
5. How is God revealed in today's reading, and what does this mean for your life?

## Answers, Ponderings, and New Discoveries:

_____
_____
_____
_____
_____
_____
_____
_____
_____
_____
_____
_____

**Prayer Requests / Answers :** _____
_____
_____
_____

## What is God doing around you, and how can you join Him?

_____
_____
_____

## Together Challenge:

Talk with someone about how you know you are a child of God.

## Daily Reading:

Genesis 4:1-26, 1 John 3:11-24

## Study Journal Question:

1. Why did God say that the one who hates his brother is a murderer?
2. Why do people hate other people, or why don't people love each other all the time?
3. How do we love in deed and in truth?
4. What are the things you can do every day to lay down your life as Jesus did?
5. How is God revealed in today's reading, and what does this mean for your life?

## Answers, Ponderings, and New Discoveries:

_____
_____
_____
_____
_____
_____
_____
_____
_____
_____
_____
_____

**Prayer Requests / Answers :** _____
_____
_____

## What is God doing around you, and how can you join Him?

_____
_____
_____

## Together Challenge:

Lay down your life for someone else today.

# Daily Reading:

Genesis 5:1-32, 1 John 4:1-6

# Study Journal Question:

1. Do you go to scripture or to the world when looking for answers to life's questions?  Why?
2. What is the significance of Seth being born in the likeness of Adam?
3. How do we "test the spirits"?
4. How does it affect your walk / life knowing that He who is in you is greater than he who is in the world?
5. How is God revealed in today's reading, and what does this mean for your life?

# Answers, Ponderings, and New Discoveries:

_____
_____
_____
_____
_____
_____
_____
_____
_____
_____

**Prayer Requests / Answers :** _____

_____
_____
_____

# What is God doing around you, and how can you join Him?

_____
_____
_____

# Together Challenge:

Make a list of people you know that listen to God and use that list next time you are seeking answers instead of asking the world.

## Daily Reading:

Genesis 6:1-22, 1 Chronicles 1:1-4

## Study Journal Question:

1. How have you grieved the heart of God?
2. What does it mean to find favor in the eyes of the Lord?
3. God gave Noah specific instructions to guide him in building the ark. How does God guide you?
4. In what ways did God provide for Noah physically, emotionally, and spiritually?
5. In what ways does God provide for you?
6. How is God revealed in today's reading, and what does this mean for your life?

## Answers, Ponderings, and New Discoveries:

_____
_____
_____
_____
_____
_____
_____
_____
_____
_____
_____

**Prayer Requests / Answers :** _____
_____
_____
_____

## What is God doing around you, and how can you join Him?

_____
_____
_____

## Together Challenge:

Take the opportunity to meet someone's needs with something God has provided for you.

## Daily Reading:

Genesis 7:1-8:22

## Study Journal Question:

1. What should your response be toward those who are figuratively outside of the Ark today?
2. Why did God send the flood, and what does it show about His view of sin?
3. Why did God vow not to destroy every living creature with a flood again?
4. What can we learn from Noah's obedience in building the ark?
5. How is God revealed in today's reading, and what does this mean for your life?

## Answers, Ponderings, and New Discoveries:

_____
_____
_____
_____
_____
_____
_____
_____
_____
_____
_____

**Prayer Requests / Answers :** _____

_____
_____
_____

## What is God doing around you, and how can you join Him?

_____
_____
_____

## Together Challenge:

Consider your relationships and choose someone to intentionally pull toward the Ark.

## Daily Reading:

Genesis 9:1-10:1, 1 John 4:7-21

## Study Journal Question:

1. What is symbolized in the covenant of the rainbow?
2. What can you learn from Ham's poor choice?
3. What does it mean to abide in God?
4. What should our response be to the love of God?
5. How is God revealed in today's reading, and what does this mean for your life?

## Answers, Ponderings, and New Discoveries:

_____
_____
_____
_____
_____
_____
_____
_____
_____
_____
_____
_____

**Prayer Requests / Answers :** _____
_____
_____
_____

## What is God doing around you, and how can you join Him?

_____
_____
_____

## Together Challenge:

Think of someone who is difficult to love, and purpose to show them love today.

## Daily Reading:

Genesis 10:2-20, 1 Chronicles 1:5-7, 1 John 5:1-21

## Study Journal Question:

1. What can we learn about the origin of nations from this genealogy?
2. Why are God's commands not burdensome or grievous?
3. What did John write to inform people that they have eternal life?
4. How do people overcome the world?
5. How is God revealed in today's reading, and what does this mean for your life?

## Answers, Ponderings, and New Discoveries:

_____
_____
_____
_____
_____
_____
_____
_____
_____
_____
_____
_____

**Prayer Requests / Answers :** _____

_____
_____

## What is God doing around you, and how can you join Him?

_____
_____
_____

## Together Challenge:

Pray with someone who has committed a sin that doesn't lead to death.

## Daily Reading:

Genesis 10:21-30, 1 Chronicles 1:8-23, John 1:1-18, Luke 1:1-4

## Study Journal Question:

1. How does the grace and truth that came through Jesus differ from the law that came through Moses?
2. Describe who God gave the right to become children of God?
3. What is the Gospel of Luke?
4. Who is the Word, and how is it described?
5. How is God revealed in today's reading, and what does this mean for your life?

## Answers, Ponderings, and New Discoveries:

_____
_____
_____
_____
_____
_____
_____
_____
_____
_____
_____
_____

**Prayer Requests / Answers :** _____

_____
_____
_____

## What is God doing around you, and how can you join Him?

_____
_____
_____

## Together Challenge:

Choose someone to bear witness to about the light (Jesus) today.

## Daily Reading:

Genesis 10:31-11:26, Matthew 1:1-17

## Study Journal Question:

1. What can we observe about God's faithfulness to Abraham, Isaac, and Jacob in the genealogies?
2. James 4 reads, "God opposes the proud." How is this illustrated in Genesis 11?
3. What is the meaning of the name Babel? What is the significance of the meaning?
4. Later in history what does Babel become known as, and what is significant about it?
5. How is God revealed in today's reading, and what does this mean for your life?

## Answers, Ponderings, and New Discoveries:

_____
_____
_____
_____
_____
_____
_____
_____
_____
_____
_____
_____

**Prayer Requests / Answers :** _____
_____
_____
_____

## What is God doing around you, and how can you join Him?

_____
_____
_____

## Together Challenge:

Take some time to consider what you are trying to accomplish with other people and ask God if it is pleasing to Him.

## Daily Reading:

Genesis 11:27-12:20, 1 Chronicles 1:24-27, Luke 3:23-38

## Study Journal Question:

1. What is the summation or completions of all the genealogy records from the Bible that are pulled together in Luke?
2. What promises did God make to Abraham?
3. How does God protect Sarai despite her husband's weakness?
4. What can we learn from God's timing in fulfilling His promises to Abraham?
5. How is God revealed in today's reading, and what does this mean for your life?

## Answers, Ponderings, and New Discoveries:

_____
_____
_____
_____
_____
_____
_____
_____
_____
_____

**Prayer Requests / Answers :** _____
_____
_____

## What is God doing around you, and how can you join Him?

_____
_____
_____

## Together Challenge:

Abraham's father and nephew supported him in his calling. Find someone you can encourage in their God-given calling.

    

## Daily Reading:

Genesis 13:1-14:16

## Study Journal Question:

1. What can we learn from Abraham's way of dealing with conflict?
2. In what ways did Abraham trust God in dealing with Lot?
3. Why did Lot choose the Jordan Valley? Should he have considered other factors as well?
4. How can you trust God when facing conflict?
5. How is God revealed in today's reading, and what does this mean for your life?

## Answers, Ponderings, and New Discoveries:

_____

_____

_____

_____

_____

_____

_____

_____

_____

_____

_____

**Prayer Requests / Answers :** _____

_____

_____

_____

## What is God doing around you, and how can you join Him?

_____

_____

_____

## Together Challenge:

Make an active effort to assist someone you know who is in a difficult season in life.

## Daily Reading:

Genesis 14:17-15:21

## Study Journal Question:

1. In Genesis 15:6, what did it mean for Abraham to believe?
2. What can we learn about God's character in that He didn't give Abraham the land immediately?
3. Why did Abraham not want to be made rich by the king of Sodom?
4. How does Hebrews 7 describe the significance of Abraham's interactions with Melchizedek?
5. How is God revealed in today's reading, and what does this mean for your life?

## Answers, Ponderings, and New Discoveries:

_____
_____
_____
_____
_____
_____
_____
_____
_____
_____
_____
_____
_____

**Prayer Requests / Answers :** _____
_____
_____
_____

## What is God doing around you, and how can you join Him?

_____
_____
_____

## Together Challenge:

Encourage someone to believe a promise God has made to us.

## Daily Reading:

Genesis 16:1-17:27, Luke 1:5-25

## Study Journal Question:

1. What are the similarities between Abraham and Zechariah's responses to their wives bearing a child?
2. What was Abraham's part, and what was God's part in the covenant that was established?
3. What is the significance of the names that God chose for people?
4. How do you respond when God calls you to do something?
5. How is God revealed in today's reading, and what does this mean for your life?

## Answers, Ponderings, and New Discoveries:

_____
_____
_____
_____
_____
_____
_____
_____
_____
_____
_____
_____

**Prayer Requests / Answers :** _____
_____
_____
_____

## What is God doing around you, and how can you join Him?

_____
_____
_____

## Together Challenge:

Listen to the cry of someone who has been rejected recently.

## Daily Reading:

Genesis 18:1-33, Luke 1:26-38

## Study Journal Question:

1. How did Abraham respond when he saw the Lord approaching and how should we walk knowing God is always with us?
2. What can we learn about God's mercy and patience from Abraham's conversation with the Lord regarding Sodom and Gomorrah?
3. In what ways were Elizabeth's and Mary's reactions similar?
4. How have you lacked in the belief that all things are possible with God?
5. How is God revealed in today's reading, and what does this mean for your life?

## Answers, Ponderings, and New Discoveries:

_____
_____
_____
_____
_____
_____
_____
_____
_____
_____

**Prayer Requests / Answers :** _____
_____
_____
_____

## What is God doing around you, and how can you join Him?

_____
_____
_____

## Together Challenge:

Find someone you can honor today.

## Daily Reading:

Genesis 19:1-29, Luke 1:39-56

## Study Journal Question:

1. What did the angels find when they went to the city?
2. Why did God save Lot and his family from the city?
3. What can we learn from God choosing Mary to bear the Christ?
4. When God leads you, do you respond more like Mary or Lot's wife?  Give an example.
5. How is God revealed in today's reading, and what does this mean for your life?

## Answers, Ponderings, and New Discoveries:

_____
_____
_____
_____
_____
_____
_____
_____
_____
_____
_____
_____

**Prayer Requests / Answers :** _____
_____
_____
_____

## What is God doing around you, and how can you join Him?

_____
_____
_____

## Together Challenge:

Give someone the courage to flee from wickedness today.

## Daily Reading:

Genesis 19:30-20:18, Proverbs 4:1-13, James 1:1-18

## Study Journal Question:

1. How did God help Abraham when he lacked faith, and how has God helped you when you lacked faith?
2. Why is wisdom valuable, and how do you get it?
3. How does temptation lead to death?
4. Why are trials an important part of our Christian life?
5. How is God revealed in today's reading, and what does this mean for your life?

## Answers, Ponderings, and New Discoveries:

_____
_____
_____
_____
_____
_____
_____
_____
_____
_____
_____
_____

**Prayer Requests / Answers :** _____
_____
_____
_____

## What is God doing around you, and how can you join Him?

_____
_____
_____

## Together Challenge:

Be a voice that encourages someone to trust God in the midst of facing a trial.

       

## Daily Reading:

Proverbs 17:1-28, James 1:19-27

## Study Journal Question:

1. What do Proverbs and James both communicate about being careful concerning what we say?
2. What does it look like in your life to be a doer of the word?
3. What is the effect of reproof or rebuke on a wise person and how do these affect you? Why?
4. How does a joyful heart impact everyone around it?
5. How is God revealed in today's reading, and what does this mean for your life?

## Answers, Ponderings, and New Discoveries:

_____
_____
_____
_____
_____
_____
_____
_____
_____
_____
_____

**Prayer Requests / Answers :** _____
_____
_____
_____

## What is God doing around you, and how can you join Him?

_____
_____
_____

## Together Challenge:

Spend some time with a widow and look for an opportunity to serve her.

## Daily Reading:

Genesis 21:1-34

## Study Journal Question:

1. How did God accomplish His purposes with Sarah's jealousy?
2. Ishmael's name means God hears. How do we see this fulfilled in the scriptures?
3. What can we learn from Abraham's interaction with Abimelech and Phicol?
4. How has God used you despite your weaknesses?
5. How is God revealed in today's reading, and what does this mean for your life?

## Answers, Ponderings, and New Discoveries:

_____
_____
_____
_____
_____
_____
_____
_____
_____
_____
_____

**Prayer Requests / Answers :** _____
_____
_____
_____

## What is God doing around you, and how can you join Him?

_____
_____
_____

## Together Challenge:

Encourage someone to know that God hears their prayers.

## Daily Reading:

Proverbs 15:1-33

## Study Journal Question:

1. What are the characteristics of the wicked?
2. How does Proverbs describe the speach of the wise?
3. How does God respond to the wicked?
4. What does it mean for the fear of the Lord to be the instruction of wisdom?
5. How is God revealed in today's reading, and what does this mean for your life?

## Answers, Ponderings, and New Discoveries:

_____
_____
_____
_____
_____
_____
_____
_____
_____
_____
_____
_____

**Prayer Requests / Answers :** _____

_____
_____
_____

## What is God doing around you, and how can you join Him?

_____
_____
_____

## Together Challenge:

Ask someone for counsel on something you are planning today.

## Daily Reading:

Genesis 22:1-24, James 2:1-26

## Study Journal Question:

1. How is 'Abraham offering Isaac on an altar' an example of both faith and works?
2. How does God respond to Abraham's faith?
3. Why is faith without works dead?
4. How do you treat people who have a different financial status than you?
5. How is God revealed in today's reading, and what does this mean for your life?

## Answers, Ponderings, and New Discoveries:

_____
_____
_____
_____
_____
_____
_____
_____
_____
_____
_____
_____

**Prayer Requests / Answers :** _____

_____
_____
_____

## What is God doing around you, and how can you join Him?

_____
_____
_____

## Together Challenge:

Minister to the physical needs of someone in your church or community.

# Daily Reading:

Proverbs 10:1-32, James 3:1-18

# Study Journal Question:

1. How does the way of the Lord bring protection to the righteous and destroy the evil doer?
2. How can you tell if your wisdom is from above?
3. What can we discern about our character and heart from the words that come out of our mouths?
4. How have your words changed the course of your life?
5. How is God revealed in today's reading, and what does this mean for your life?

# Answers, Ponderings, and New Discoveries:

_____
_____
_____
_____
_____
_____
_____
_____
_____
_____
_____

**Prayer Requests / Answers :** _____
_____
_____
_____

# What is God doing around you, and how can you join Him?

_____
_____
_____

# Together Challenge:

Since teachers are going to be judged more strictly, pick one to pray for today.

## Daily Reading:

Genesis 23:1-20, Psalm 138:1-8, James 4:1-17

## Study Journal Question:

1. How does God respond to humility and pride?
2. How would it affect the way you plan for the future if you did it saying, "if the Lord wills"?
3. Why don't people get what they want?
4. How do we overcome the Devil?
5. How is God revealed in today's reading, and what does this mean for your life?

## Answers, Ponderings, and New Discoveries:

_____
_____
_____
_____
_____
_____
_____
_____
_____
_____
_____
_____

**Prayer Requests / Answers :** _____
_____
_____
_____

## What is God doing around you, and how can you join Him?

_____
_____
_____

## Together Challenge:

Life is but a vapor. Comfort someone who has lost a loved one.

## Daily Reading:

Proverbs 13:1-25, James 5:1-12

## Study Journal Question:

1. How is our waiting for the coming of the Lord similar to a farmer waiting?
2. How have you experienced God's compassion and mercy?
3. How is discipline an act of love?
4. How are we affected by our companions and the people we talk with?
5. How is God revealed in today's reading, and what does this mean for your life?

## Answers, Ponderings, and New Discoveries:

_____
_____
_____
_____
_____
_____
_____
_____
_____
_____
_____
_____

**Prayer Requests / Answers :** _____
_____
_____
_____

## What is God doing around you, and how can you join Him?

_____
_____
_____

## Together Challenge:

If you owe someone and have the money, pay them today.

## Daily Reading:

Psalm 107:1-43, James 5:13-20

## Study Journal Question:

1. How does God respond to our prayers and cries to Him when we are in trouble?
2. How has God specifically helped you in difficult situations?
3. What does it look like to give thanks and praise to the Lord?
4. Why is it important for us to turn sinners from their wanderings? How are you living this out?
5. How is God revealed in today's reading, and what does this mean for your life?

## Answers, Ponderings, and New Discoveries:

_____
_____
_____
_____
_____
_____
_____
_____
_____
_____
_____
_____

**Prayer Requests / Answers :** _____
_____
_____
_____

## What is God doing around you, and how can you join Him?

_____
_____
_____

## Together Challenge:

Pray with someone who is sick or in trouble.

    

## Daily Reading:

Genesis 24:1-28

## Study Journal Question:

1. How did God lead Abraham's servant, and how does God direct you?
2. How did Rebeka's response to the servant reflect her character?
3. Why did Abraham tell his servant not to bring his son back to the land of his kindred?
4. When it comes to finding a spouse, how does our culture differ from Isaac's?
5. How is God revealed in today's reading, and what does this mean for your life?

## Answers, Ponderings, and New Discoveries:

_____
_____
_____
_____
_____
_____
_____
_____
_____
_____
_____

**Prayer Requests / Answers :** _____
_____
_____
_____

## What is God doing around you, and how can you join Him?

_____
_____
_____

## Together Challenge:

When at work or at home and someone asks you to do something, go the extra mile in serving them.

## Daily Reading:

Genesis 24:29-67

## Study Journal Question:

1. How did Bethuel's household treat Abraham's servant?
2. How did Rebeka's family respond to Abraham's servant's request?
3. What was the purpose of all the gifts that Abraham's servant gave?
4. In what ways can you pray like Abraham's servant?
5. How is God revealed in today's reading, and what does this mean for your life?

## Answers, Ponderings, and New Discoveries:

_____
_____
_____
_____
_____
_____
_____
_____
_____
_____
_____
_____

**Prayer Requests / Answers :** _____

_____
_____
_____

## What is God doing around you, and how can you join Him?

_____
_____
_____

## Together Challenge:

Show hospitality to a servant of the Lord today.

## Daily Reading:

Genesis 25:1-26, 1 Chronicles 1:28-34, Luke 1:57-66

## Study Journal Question:

1. Why did Abraham give Isaac all that he had?
2. Have you ever prayed for something like Issac? What did God do?
3. Why were Rebekah's children struggling within her?
4. Why was Zachariah's mouth opened and his tongue loosed?
5. How is God revealed in today's reading, and what does this mean for your life?

## Answers, Ponderings, and New Discoveries:

_____
_____
_____
_____
_____
_____
_____
_____
_____
_____
_____

**Prayer Requests / Answers :** _____
_____
_____
_____

## What is God doing around you, and how can you join Him?

_____
_____
_____

## Together Challenge:

Rejoice with someone who has received a blessing from God.

## Daily Reading:

Genesis 25:27-26:35, Luke 1:67-80

## Study Journal Question:

1. What did Esau give up for a bowl of stew?
2. How did Abimelech's past experiences with Abraham affect his response to Isaac's lie?
3. How did Abraham's faithfulness to God impact Issac's life and future?
4. What did Zachariah prophesy about John's purpose?
5. How is God revealed in today's reading, and what does this mean for your life?

## Answers, Ponderings, and New Discoveries:

_____
_____
_____
_____
_____
_____
_____
_____
_____
_____
_____
_____
_____

**Prayer Requests / Answers :** _____
_____
_____
_____

## What is God doing around you, and how can you join Him?

_____
_____
_____

## Together Challenge:

Find a way to make peace in a difficult relationship by being selfless.

        

# Daily Reading:

Genesis 27:1-40, Matthew 1:18-25

# Study Journal Question:

1. Why did Jacob and Rebekah deceive Isaac?
2. How was Esau's reaction to losing his blessing different from losing his birthright?
3. How does the meaning of the names Jesus and Immanuel define who He is?
4. What is the difference in Joseph's response before and after his dream?
5. How is God revealed in today's reading, and what does this mean for your life?

# Answers, Ponderings, and New Discoveries:

_____
_____
_____
_____
_____
_____
_____
_____
_____
_____
_____
_____
_____

**Prayer Requests / Answers :** _____
_____
_____
_____

# What is God doing around you, and how can you join Him?

_____
_____
_____

# Together Challenge:

Contact someone today and pronounce a blessing over them.

## Daily Reading:

Genesis 27:41-28:22, Luke 2:1-7

## Study Journal Question:

1. Why did Rebeka send Jacob away?
2. Why did God choose Jacob to fulfill His promise to Abraham?
3. What did God promise Jacob?
4. Why was Jesus born in Bethlehem?
5. How is God revealed in today's reading, and what does this mean for your life?

## Answers, Ponderings, and New Discoveries:

_____
_____
_____
_____
_____
_____
_____
_____
_____
_____
_____
_____

**Prayer Requests / Answers :** _____
_____
_____
_____

## What is God doing around you, and how can you join Him?

_____
_____
_____

## Together Challenge:

Jacob set up a pillar after God made a promise to his family. Set up a reminder for your family to help them remember God's promises.

## Daily Reading:

Genesis 29:1-30, Luke 2:8-20

## Study Journal Question:

1. What character qualities did Laban and his sister Rebeka have in common?
2. How did Laban treat his daughters?
3. What was communicated to the shepherds?
4. How did Mary respond to the shepherds?
5. How is God revealed in today's reading, and what does this mean for your life?

## Answers, Ponderings, and New Discoveries:

_____
_____
_____
_____
_____
_____
_____
_____
_____
_____
_____
_____

**Prayer Requests / Answers :** _____
_____
_____

## What is God doing around you, and how can you join Him?

_____
_____
_____

## Together Challenge:

Glorify and praise God with someone else today.

## Daily Reading:

Genesis 29:31-30:24

## Study Journal Question:

1. What was it like for Jacob to have more than one wife?
2. What value did Jacob's family place on having children?
3. What was Rachel and Leah's relationship like?
4. Have you ever been jealous of someone? Why?
5. How is God revealed in today's reading, and what does this mean for your life?

## Answers, Ponderings, and New Discoveries:

_____
_____
_____
_____
_____
_____
_____
_____
_____
_____
_____

**Prayer Requests / Answers :** _____
_____
_____
_____

## What is God doing around you, and how can you join Him?

_____
_____
_____

## Together Challenge:

Deal with jealousy toward others by recognizing that you don't deserve anything.

## Daily Reading:

Genesis 30:25-31:21

## Study Journal Question:

1. How did God protect Jacob from Laban?
2. What was Leah and Rachel's reaction to Jacob's proposal to leave?
3. How did Laban treat Jacob?
4. In your relationships, are you more like Laban or Jacob?
5. How is God revealed in today's reading, and what does this mean for your life?

## Answers, Ponderings, and New Discoveries:

_____
_____
_____
_____
_____
_____
_____
_____
_____
_____
_____
_____

**Prayer Requests / Answers :** _____

_____
_____
_____

## What is God doing around you, and how can you join Him?

_____
_____
_____

## Together Challenge:

Don't cheat anyone who does work for you, but pay them what they are due.

## Daily Reading:

Genesis 31:22-55, Luke 2:21-40

## Study Journal Question:

1. Why didn't Laban hurt Jacob?
2. Why were Jacob and Laban mad at each other?
3. Jacob and Laban came to peaceful terms. How can you make peace with someone who has done you wrong?
4. What was Simeon and Anna's response to seeing Jesus?
5. How is God revealed in today's reading, and what does this mean for your life?

## Answers, Ponderings, and New Discoveries:

_____
_____
_____
_____
_____
_____
_____
_____
_____
_____
_____

**Prayer Requests / Answers :** _____
_____
_____
_____

## What is God doing around you, and how can you join Him?

_____
_____
_____

## Together Challenge:

Make peace with someone who has wronged you.

## Daily Reading:

Genesis 32:1-32, Matthew 2:1-12

## Study Journal Question:

1. Why didn't Jacob run away from Esau?
2. What is the meaning of Jacob and Israel?
3. What does it look like for you to wrestle with God?
4. What is the significance of the wise men coming?
5. How is God revealed in today's reading, and what does this mean for your life?

## Answers, Ponderings, and New Discoveries:

_____
_____
_____
_____
_____
_____
_____
_____
_____
_____
_____

**Prayer Requests / Answers :** _____
_____
_____
_____

## What is God doing around you, and how can you join Him?

_____
_____
_____

## Together Challenge:

Honor someone with a gift today.

## Daily Reading:

Genesis 33:1-20, Matthew 2:13-23

## Study Journal Question:

1. How did Jacob and Esau respond to each other?
2. Why didn't Jacob go with Esau?
3. How were the prophecies about Jesus fulfilled?
4. How have you forgiven someone who has wronged you?
5. How is God revealed in today's reading, and what does this mean for your life?

## Answers, Ponderings, and New Discoveries:

_____
_____
_____
_____
_____
_____
_____
_____
_____
_____
_____

**Prayer Requests / Answers :** _____

_____
_____
_____

## What is God doing around you, and how can you join Him?

_____
_____
_____

## Together Challenge:

Ask forgiveness from someone you have wronged in your past.

## Daily Reading:

Genesis 34:1-31, Luke 2:41-52

## Study Journal Question:

1. How did Jacob respond differently than his son's to Shechem?
2. How did Jacob's sons deceive Shechem and his people?
3. Why wasn't justice accomplished by Simeon and Levi's revenge?
4. How was Jesus different from most 12-year-olds?
5. How is God revealed in today's reading, and what does this mean for your life?

## Answers, Ponderings, and New Discoveries:

_____
_____
_____
_____
_____
_____
_____
_____
_____
_____
_____
_____

**Prayer Requests / Answers :** _____
_____
_____
_____

**What is God doing around you, and how can you join Him?**

_____
_____
_____

## Together Challenge:

Engage other Christians in conversation where you are both listening and asking questions about spiritual truths.

## Daily Reading:

Genesis 35:1-29, Mark 1:1-8

## Study Journal Question:

1. What did God promise Jacob?
2. How and where did Rachel die?
3. What would it mean for you to put away foreign Gods?
4. What was John the Baptist's message?
5. How is God revealed in today's reading, and what does this mean for your life?

## Answers, Ponderings, and New Discoveries:

_____
_____
_____
_____
_____
_____
_____
_____
_____
_____
_____

**Prayer Requests / Answers :** _____
_____
_____
_____

## What is God doing around you, and how can you join Him?

_____
_____
_____

## Together Challenge:

Prepare an unbeliever for Jesus by proclaiming repentance and forgiveness of sins.

## Daily Reading:

Genesis 36:1-30, 1 Chronicles 1:35-37

## Study Journal Question:

1. Why did Esau move to Seir instead of Jacob?
2. Why are genealogies in the Bible?
3. How can you relate to Jacob's weaknesses that we read about this last week?
4. What have you learned about Jacob and Esau's character this last week?
5. How is God revealed in today's reading, and what does this mean for your life?

## Answers, Ponderings, and New Discoveries:

_____
_____
_____
_____
_____
_____
_____
_____
_____
_____
_____
_____

**Prayer Requests / Answers :** _____

_____
_____

## What is God doing around you, and how can you join Him?

_____
_____
_____

## Together Challenge:

Encourage someone that if God can work with a man like Jacob, He can work with them too.

## Daily Reading:

Genesis 36:31-43, 1 Chronicles 1:38-2:2

## Study Journal Question:

1. What is the most profound thing you have learned since you started this study?
2. Who can you ask to join you in reading the Bible?
3. What opportunities do you have to share with others what you are learning?
4. How can you be a Christian influence in your circle of relationships?
5. How is God revealed in today's reading, and what does this mean for your life?

## Answers, Ponderings, and New Discoveries:

_____
_____
_____
_____
_____
_____
_____
_____
_____
_____
_____
_____

**Prayer Requests / Answers :** _____
_____
_____
_____

## What is God doing around you, and how can you join Him?

_____
_____
_____

## Together Challenge:

Initiate a spiritual conversation with someone by asking them a question.

## Daily Reading:

Genesis 37:1-36, Luke 3:1-18

## Study Journal Question:

1. How does a father favoring one child create conflict among siblings?
2. How did Reuben's intent for Joseph differ from Judah's?
3. How has jealousy affected relationships in your family?
4. How did John the Baptist teach others to live?
5. How is God revealed in today's reading, and what does this mean for your life?

## Answers, Ponderings, and New Discoveries:

_____
_____
_____
_____
_____
_____
_____
_____
_____
_____
_____
_____

**Prayer Requests / Answers :** _____
_____
_____
_____

## What is God doing around you, and how can you join Him?

_____
_____
_____

## Together Challenge:

Share food and clothing with someone in need today.

## Daily Reading:

Genesis 38:1-30, 1 Chronicles 2:3-8, Matthew 3:1-12

## Study Journal Question:

1. What can we learn about who God uses knowing that Judah and Tamar were part of the genealogy of Christ?
2. How has God used your sins to accomplish His purposes?
3. What were the hearts of the people like that went to hear John the Baptist?
4. What did John say would happen to those who repented but didn't bear fruit?
5. How is God revealed in today's reading, and what does this mean for your life?

## Answers, Ponderings, and New Discoveries:

_____
_____
_____
_____
_____
_____
_____
_____
_____
_____
_____
_____

**Prayer Requests / Answers :** _____
_____
_____
_____

## What is God doing around you, and how can you join Him?

_____
_____
_____

## Together Challenge:

Tell someone how they can escape the wrath of God.

## Daily Reading:

Genesis 39:1-23, Matthew 3:13-17, Mark 1:9-11

## Study Journal Question:

1. Why did those around Joseph find favor in him?
2. How did Joseph respond to temptation? How do you respond to temptation?
3. What skills did Joseph learn while a slave and in prison?
4. What did God declare about Jesus?
5. How is God revealed in today's reading, and what does this mean for your life?

## Answers, Ponderings, and New Discoveries:

_____
_____
_____
_____
_____
_____
_____
_____
_____
_____
_____
_____

**Prayer Requests / Answers :** _____
_____
_____
_____

## What is God doing around you, and how can you join Him?

_____
_____
_____

## Together Challenge:

Encourage someone to flee temptation.

## Daily Reading:

Genesis 40:1-23, Luke 3:21-22, Mark 1:12-13

## Study Journal Question:

1. How does it feel to be forgotten or rejected?
2. Who led Jesus into the wilderness?
3. How did God use Joseph while in prison?
4. What is the significance that God now calls us beloved?
5. How is God revealed in today's reading, and what does this mean for your life?

## Answers, Ponderings, and New Discoveries:

_____
_____
_____
_____
_____
_____
_____
_____
_____
_____
_____
_____

**Prayer Requests / Answers :** _____
_____
_____
_____

## What is God doing around you, and how can you join Him?

_____
_____
_____

## Together Challenge:

Encourage someone who feels forgotten.

## Daily Reading:

Genesis 41:1-24, Matthew 4:1-11, Psalm 91:1-16

## Study Journal Question:

1. What evidence is there that Joseph still trusted God?
2. How long did it take for the cupbearer to remember Joseph? What can we learn about God's timing from this?
3. How did Satan use the truth to tempt Jesus?
4. What can we learn from Jesus' example about how to apply Psalm 91 to our lives?
5. How is God revealed in today's reading, and what does this mean for your life?

## Answers, Ponderings, and New Discoveries:

_____
_____
_____
_____
_____
_____
_____
_____
_____
_____
_____

**Prayer Requests / Answers :** _____
_____
_____
_____

## What is God doing around you, and how can you join Him?

_____
_____
_____

## Together Challenge:

Honor someone who has helped you in the past.

## Daily Reading:

Genesis 41:25-57

## Study Journal Question:

1. What did Pharaoh's dream mean?
2. How did God prepare Joseph to be qualified to be an overseer?
3. How has God prepared you for where you are at right now?
4. What can we infer about Joseph's heart in naming his son Manasseh?
5. How is God revealed in today's reading, and what does this mean for your life?

## Answers, Ponderings, and New Discoveries:

_____
_____
_____
_____
_____
_____
_____
_____
_____
_____
_____

**Prayer Requests / Answers :** _____
_____
_____
_____

## What is God doing around you, and how can you join Him?

_____
_____
_____

## Together Challenge:

Bring groceries to a family whom you know is in need.

## Daily Reading:

Genesis 42:1-38

## Study Journal Question:

1. How was Benjamin's relationship with his father different from the rest of his brothers'?
2. How did Joseph try to reveal his brothers' hearts?
3. How did Joseph's dreams from the past unfold?
4. How would you respond if you were in Joseph's position?
5. How is God revealed in today's reading, and what does this mean for your life?

## Answers, Ponderings, and New Discoveries:

_____
_____
_____
_____
_____
_____
_____
_____
_____
_____
_____
_____

**Prayer Requests / Answers :** _____
_____
_____
_____

## What is God doing around you, and how can you join Him?

_____
_____
_____

## Together Challenge:

Show compassion toward someone who has wronged you.

## Daily Reading:

Genesis 43:1-34, Luke 4:1-15

## Study Journal Question:

1. How did Jacob's sons feel about going back to face Joseph?
2. How did Joseph react to his brothers' return?
3. How did Jesus use scripture in His interactions with the devil?
4. How can you prepare your heart to fight temptation like Jesus did?
5. How is God revealed in today's reading, and what does this mean for your life?

## Answers, Ponderings, and New Discoveries:

_____
_____
_____
_____
_____
_____
_____
_____
_____
_____
_____
_____

**Prayer Requests / Answers :** _____
_____
_____
_____

## What is God doing around you, and how can you join Him?

_____
_____
_____

## Together Challenge:

Show honor to someone who is in a leadership position.

## Daily Reading:

Genesis 44:1-34, John 1:19-34

## Study Journal Question:

1. How was Judah's response toward Benjamin different from how he treated Joseph as a young man?
2. Why did Joseph have the silver cup placed in Benjamin's sack? What did it reveal about his brothers' hearts?
3. What did John say about Jesus?
4. How has God revealed who Jesus is to you?
5. How is God revealed in today's reading, and what does this mean for your life?

## Answers, Ponderings, and New Discoveries:

_____
_____
_____
_____
_____
_____
_____
_____
_____
_____
_____

**Prayer Requests / Answers :** _____
_____
_____
_____

## What is God doing around you, and how can you join Him?

_____
_____
_____

## Together Challenge:

Show honor to your father in spite of his mistakes.

## Daily Reading:

Genesis 45:1-28, John 1:35-51

## Study Journal Question:

1. How did Joseph view what his brothers did to him?
2. What did Joseph offer his father and brothers?
3. How did Jesus meet the men that would become His disciples?
4. What was your first encounter with Jesus like?
5. How is God revealed in today's reading, and what does this mean for your life?

## Answers, Ponderings, and New Discoveries:

_____
_____
_____
_____
_____
_____
_____
_____
_____
_____
_____
_____

**Prayer Requests / Answers :** _____
_____
_____
_____

## What is God doing around you, and how can you join Him?

_____
_____
_____

## Together Challenge:

Introduce a friend to Jesus.

## Daily Reading:

Genesis 46:1-34, John 2:1-12

## Study Journal Question:

**1.** How did God remind Jacob of His promise to him?

**2.** How did Israel and Joseph respond to seeing each other?

**3.** Who witnessed Jesus' miracle, and what was their reaction?

**4.** What miracles has God performed in your life?

**5.** How is God revealed in today's reading, and what does this mean for your life?

## Answers, Ponderings, and New Discoveries:

_____
_____
_____
_____
_____
_____
_____
_____
_____
_____
_____
_____

**Prayer Requests / Answers :** _____
_____
_____
_____

## What is God doing around you, and how can you join Him?

_____
_____
_____

## Together Challenge:

Reach out to a friend or family member with whom connection has been broken.

## Daily Reading:
Genesis 47:1-31, John 2:13-25

## Study Journal Question:

1. What did Joseph accomplish for Pharaoh?
2. How did God provide for Jacob and his family?
3. How did Jesus fulfill the prophecy, "zeal for your house will consume me"?
4. How has scripture that you have read come alive at a later time in your walk with the Lord?
5. How is God revealed in today's reading, and what does this mean for your life?

## Answers, Ponderings, and New Discoveries:

_____
_____
_____
_____
_____
_____
_____
_____
_____
_____
_____
_____

**Prayer Requests / Answers :** _____
_____
_____
_____

## What is God doing around you, and how can you join Him?
_____
_____
_____

## Together Challenge:

Discuss today's study questions with a friend.

## Daily Reading:

Genesis 48:1-22

## Study Journal Question:

1. What is unique about Joseph's sons compared to his brother's children?
2. Why did Joseph bring his sons to their grandfather?
3. What are the similarities between the blessing Jacob received from God and the blessing Jacob gave to Manasseh and Ephraim?
4. How have you experienced the blessing of God in your life?
5. How is God revealed in today's reading, and what does this mean for your life?

## Answers, Ponderings, and New Discoveries:

_____
_____
_____
_____
_____
_____
_____
_____
_____
_____
_____

**Prayer Requests / Answers :** _____
_____
_____
_____

## What is God doing around you, and how can you join Him?

_____
_____
_____

## Together Challenge:

Visit someone who is ill.

## Daily Reading:

Genesis 49:1-28

## Study Journal Question:

1. How did Jacob's sons' past actions affect the blessing they received?
2. What is unique about Judah's blessing compared to his brothers'?
3. How was Joseph's blessing a reflection of his life?
4. Based on the life you live right now, what kind of blessing would you receive?
5. How is God revealed in today's reading, and what does this mean for your life?

## Answers, Ponderings, and New Discoveries:

_____
_____
_____
_____
_____
_____
_____
_____
_____
_____
_____
_____

**Prayer Requests / Answers :** _____
_____
_____
_____

## What is God doing around you, and how can you join Him?

_____
_____
_____

## Together Challenge:

Write a letter to inspire someone to live out God's calling for their life.

## Daily Reading:

Genesis 49:29-50:26, John 3:1-22

## Study Journal Question:

1. How did God use Jesus and Joseph to save people?

2. What is the difference between the life Jesus gives and the life preserved through Joseph?

3. What does it mean to be born again?

4. How do you know if you live in the light or the darkness?

5. How is God revealed in today's reading, and what does this mean for your life?

## Answers, Ponderings, and New Discoveries:

_____
_____
_____
_____
_____
_____
_____
_____
_____
_____
_____

**Prayer Requests / Answers :** _____
_____
_____

## What is God doing around you, and how can you join Him?

_____
_____
_____

## Together Challenge:

Empathize with someone who is experiencing a loss.

## Daily Reading:

Psalm 101:1-8, Job 1:1-22, John 3:23-36

## Study Journal Question:

1. How is Job's character reflected in Psalm 101?
2. Why did bad things happen to Job?
3. What did Job lose, and how did he respond?
4. When John lost his followers to Jesus, how did he respond?
5. How is God revealed in today's reading, and what does this mean for your life?

## Answers, Ponderings, and New Discoveries:

_____
_____
_____
_____
_____
_____
_____
_____
_____
_____
_____
_____

**Prayer Requests / Answers :** _____
_____
_____
_____

## What is God doing around you, and how can you join Him?

_____
_____
_____

## Together Challenge:

Talk with someone about how you both have responded to a loss in your past.

## Daily Reading:

Job 2:1-3:26, John 4:1-26

## Study Journal Question:

1. What authority does Satan have?
2. How can you relate to Job's wife and his friend?
3. What is living water?
4. How does the way you worship compare to the way Jesus described worship?
5. How is God revealed in today's reading, and what does this mean for your life?

## Answers, Ponderings, and New Discoveries:

_____
_____
_____
_____
_____
_____
_____
_____
_____
_____
_____

**Prayer Requests / Answers :** _____
_____
_____
_____

## What is God doing around you, and how can you join Him?

_____
_____
_____

## Together Challenge:

Listen to someone who is facing difficulties.

## Daily Reading:

Job 4:1-21, John 4:27-45, Mark 1:14-15, Luke 3:19-20

## Study Journal Question:

1. How did Eliphaz respond to Job and his situation? How would you respond?
2. In what ways did Jesus touch the Samaritan woman's heart?
3. What can you learn about the character of Jesus through His interactions with the Samaritan people?
4. What was more valuable to Jesus than food?
5. How is God revealed in today's reading, and what does this mean for your life?

## Answers, Ponderings, and New Discoveries:

_____
_____
_____
_____
_____
_____
_____
_____
_____
_____
_____
_____

**Prayer Requests / Answers :** _____
_____
_____
_____

## What is God doing around you, and how can you join Him?

_____
_____
_____

## Together Challenge:

Talk to an unbeliever about the kingdom of God.

## Daily Reading:

Job 5:1-27, Matthew 4:12-17, John 4:46-54

## Study Journal Question:

1. Why did Eliphaz think bad things were happening to Job?
2. Why did Jesus heal the official's son?
3. Where did Isaiah prophesy Jesus would come from?
4. Do you live like the kingdom of Heaven is at hand?
5. How is God revealed in today's reading, and what does this mean for your life?

## Answers, Ponderings, and New Discoveries:

_____
_____
_____
_____
_____
_____
_____
_____
_____
_____
_____
_____

**Prayer Requests / Answers :** _____
_____
_____
_____

## What is God doing around you, and how can you join Him?

_____
_____
_____

## Together Challenge:

Share with someone in your household why you believe.

## Daily Reading:

Job 6:1-7:5

## Study Journal Question:

1. In what ways was Job suffering?
2. How has physical suffering affected your spirituality?
3. What was Job's request of God?
4. What did Job ask of his friend?
5. How is God revealed in today's reading, and what does this mean for your life?

## Answers, Ponderings, and New Discoveries:

_____
_____
_____
_____
_____
_____
_____
_____
_____
_____
_____
_____

**Prayer Requests / Answers :** _____
_____
_____
_____

## What is God doing around you, and how can you join Him?

_____
_____
_____

## Together Challenge:

Pray with someone about a struggle they are experiencing.

## Daily Reading:

Job 7:6-8:22

## Study Journal Question:

1. In what ways can you relate to Job's feelings?
2. How did Bildad respond to Job?
3. How did Job question God?
4. How does Job feel about his relationship with God?
5. How is God revealed in today's reading, and what does this mean for your life?

## Answers, Ponderings, and New Discoveries:

_____
_____
_____
_____
_____
_____
_____
_____
_____
_____
_____
_____

**Prayer Requests / Answers :** _____
_____
_____
_____

## What is God doing around you, and how can you join Him?

_____
_____
_____

## Together Challenge:

Spend time with someone who is suffering.

## Daily Reading:
Job 9:1-35, Luke 4:16-30

## Study Journal Question:

1. How does Job view God's justice?
2. When you feel like you haven't been treated fairly, how do you deal with it?
3. Why did the people want to kill Jesus after He had given a gracious message to them?
4. How can we see both Jesus' compassion and blunt honesty in today's reading?
5. How is God revealed in today's reading, and what does this mean for your life?

## Answers, Ponderings, and New Discoveries:

_____
_____
_____
_____
_____
_____
_____
_____
_____
_____
_____
_____

**Prayer Requests / Answers :** _____
_____
_____
_____

## What is God doing around you, and how can you join Him?

_____
_____
_____

## Together Challenge:

Speak a message of hope to someone even if it offends them.

## Daily Reading:

Job 10:1-11:20, Matthew 4:18-22, Mark 1:16-20

## Study Journal Question:

1. What was Zophar's advice to Job?
2. How did the men respond when Jesus called them?
3. How do you respond when God calls you?
4. What does it mean to be a "fisher of men"? Are you a "fisher of men"?
5. How is God revealed in today's reading, and what does this mean for your life?

## Answers, Ponderings, and New Discoveries:

_____
_____
_____
_____
_____
_____
_____
_____
_____
_____
_____
_____

**Prayer Requests / Answers :** _____
_____
_____
_____

## What is God doing around you, and how can you join Him?

_____
_____
_____

## Together Challenge:

Encourage Christians around you to be "fishers of men".

## Daily Reading:

Job 12:1-25, Mark 1:21-28

## Study Journal Question:

1. How does Job view God's relationship with man?
2. What did it mean for Jesus to teach with authority?
3. How is the authority of God over Satan in the book of Job similar to the authority Jesus displayed over the unclean spirit?
4. How do you view God's authority?
5. How is God revealed in today's reading, and what does this mean for your life?

## Answers, Ponderings, and New Discoveries:

_____
_____
_____
_____
_____
_____
_____
_____
_____
_____
_____
_____

**Prayer Requests / Answers :** _____
_____
_____
_____

## What is God doing around you, and how can you join Him?

_____
_____
_____

## Together Challenge:

Share with someone how Jesus can set them free.

        

## Daily Reading:

Job 13:1-28, Luke 4:31-37, Mark 1:29-34

## Study Journal Question:

1. What did Job think of his friends' responses, and what did he ask them?
2. What did the demons recognize about Jesus?
3. How did the news of Jesus spread?
4. How have you experienced the healing power of Jesus?
5. How is God revealed in today's reading, and what does this mean for your life?

## Answers, Ponderings, and New Discoveries:

_____
_____
_____
_____
_____
_____
_____
_____
_____
_____
_____

**Prayer Requests / Answers :** _____
_____
_____
_____

## What is God doing around you, and how can you join Him?

_____
_____
_____

## Together Challenge:

Pray for someone who needs healing.

## Daily Reading:
Job 14:1-22, Luke 4:38-41, Matthew 8:14-17

## Study Journal Question:

1. What did Job believe will happen to people after they die?
2. How did Simon Peter's mother-in-law respond after being healed?
3. What did Jesus do to heal Simon Peter's mother-in-law?
4. How have you approached healing the sick?
5. How is God revealed in today's reading, and what does this mean for your life?

## Answers, Ponderings, and New Discoveries:

_____
_____
_____
_____
_____
_____
_____
_____
_____
_____
_____
_____

**Prayer Requests / Answers :** _____
_____
_____
_____

## What is God doing around you, and how can you join Him?

_____
_____
_____

## Together Challenge:

Talk with someone about Jesus' authority to heal.

## Daily Reading:

Job 15:1-35

## Study Journal Question:

1. What did Eliphaz think would happen to bad people?
2. What did Eliphaz think about what Job said?
3. How is Eliphaz wrong in his accusations against Job?
4. What statements spoken by Eliphaz are true?
5. How is God revealed in today's reading, and what does this mean for your life?

## Answers, Ponderings, and New Discoveries:

_____
_____
_____
_____
_____
_____
_____
_____
_____
_____
_____

**Prayer Requests / Answers :** _____
_____
_____

## What is God doing around you, and how can you join Him?

_____
_____
_____

## Together Challenge:

Use something besides words to encourage a friend.

## Daily Reading:

Job 16:1-17:16

## Study Journal Question:

1. How are people treating Job in today's reading?
2. How does Job describe his physical appearance after enduring such suffering?
3. How would you describe a time in your life when you lost hope?
4. How does Job elude to having an advocate in heaven?
5. How is God revealed in today's reading, and what does this mean for your life?

## Answers, Ponderings, and New Discoveries:

_____
_____
_____
_____
_____
_____
_____
_____
_____
_____
_____
_____

**Prayer Requests / Answers :** _____
_____
_____
_____

## What is God doing around you, and how can you join Him?

_____
_____
_____

## Together Challenge:

Give the hopeless a reason to hope.

    

## Daily Reading:
Job 18:1-21, Luke 4:42-44, Mark 1:35-39, Matthew 4:23-25

## Study Journal Question:

1. What is Bildad's understanding of what happens to the wicked?
2. Why did Jesus get away from all the people?
3. Why didn't Jesus preach in only one town?
4. How do you spread the good news of the kingdom wherever you go?
5. How is God revealed in today's reading, and what does this mean for your life?

## Answers, Ponderings, and New Discoveries:

_____
_____
_____
_____
_____
_____
_____
_____
_____
_____
_____

**Prayer Requests / Answers :** _____
_____
_____
_____

## What is God doing around you, and how can you join Him?
_____
_____
_____

## Together Challenge:

Go outside of your comfort zone to tell someone about the good news of the Kingdom.

## Daily Reading:

Job 19:1-29, Luke 5:1-11

## Study Journal Question:

1. How did Job hope in the resurrection in the midst of his difficulties?
2. In what ways did Simon display both faith and doubt?
3. How did Jesus prove to the fishermen that they could leave their boats and follow him?
4. What have you left to follow Jesus?
5. How is God revealed in today's reading, and what does this mean for your life?

## Answers, Ponderings, and New Discoveries:

_____
_____
_____
_____
_____
_____
_____
_____
_____
_____
_____
_____

**Prayer Requests / Answers :** _____
_____
_____
_____

## What is God doing around you, and how can you join Him?

_____
_____
_____

## Together Challenge:

Share a personal testimony with a new believer about how God has met your needs.

## Daily Reading:

Job 20:1-29, Luke 5:12-16, Matthew 8:1-4, Mark 1:40-45

## Study Journal Question:

1. What does Zophar think the heritage of the wicked is?
2. How did the leper express his faith in Jesus?
3. How did Jesus respond to the leper?
4. How do you respond when your request to God is answered?
5. How is God revealed in today's reading, and what does this mean for your life?

## Answers, Ponderings, and New Discoveries:

_____
_____
_____
_____
_____
_____
_____
_____
_____
_____
_____
_____

**Prayer Requests / Answers :** _____
_____
_____
_____

## What is God doing around you, and how can you join Him?

_____
_____
_____

## Together Challenge:

Tell someone about the healing God has done in your life.

## Daily Reading:

Job 21:1-34, Mark 2:1-12

## Study Journal Question:

1. What has Job observed about the wicked?
2. How does Jesus' ability to perceive what is in people's hearts affect your relationship with God?
3. How did Jesus show He could forgive sins?
4. Is your heart like the scribes and pharisees, or like the paralytic's friends? Why?
5. How is God revealed in today's reading, and what does this mean for your life?

## Answers, Ponderings, and New Discoveries:

_____
_____
_____
_____
_____
_____
_____
_____
_____
_____
_____
_____

**Prayer Requests / Answers :** _____
_____
_____
_____

## What is God doing around you, and how can you join Him?

_____
_____
_____

## Together Challenge:

Prayerfully team up with believers to bring a sinner to Jesus.

## Daily Reading:

Job 22:1-30, Matthew 9:1-8

## Study Journal Question:

1. What did Eliphaz accuse Job of doing?
2. What did Jesus do for the paralytic man?
3. How would you respond if you saw Jesus heal someone?
4. What moved Jesus to forgive the sins of the paralytic?
5. How is God revealed in today's reading, and what does this mean for your life?

## Answers, Ponderings, and New Discoveries:

_____
_____
_____
_____
_____
_____
_____
_____
_____
_____
_____

**Prayer Requests / Answers :** _____
_____
_____
_____

## What is God doing around you, and how can you join Him?

_____
_____
_____

## Together Challenge:

Choose to forgive those who have offended you.

## Daily Reading:

Job 23:1-24:25

## Study Journal Question:

1. In what ways can you relate to Job wanting to plead his case with God?
2. How does Job describe those that hide from the light?
3. When have you seen the wicked not get what they deserve?
4. How do you respond when you don't see justice served here on earth?
5. How is God revealed in today's reading, and what does this mean for your life?

## Answers, Ponderings, and New Discoveries:

_____
_____
_____
_____
_____
_____
_____
_____
_____
_____
_____
_____

**Prayer Requests / Answers :** _____
_____
_____
_____

## What is God doing around you, and how can you join Him?

_____
_____
_____

## Together Challenge:

Use love and truth to expose one hiding from the light.

## Daily Reading:

Job 25:1-27:23

## Study Journal Question:

1. How do you respond when people falsely accuse you?
2. As long as Job was alive, what did he declare that he would do?
3. How does Job describe the portion of the wicked man?
4. How would you respond to Bildad's question, "How can man be right before God?"
5. How is God revealed in today's reading, and what does this mean for your life?

## Answers, Ponderings, and New Discoveries:

_____
_____
_____
_____
_____
_____
_____
_____
_____
_____
_____

**Prayer Requests / Answers :** _____
_____
_____
_____

## What is God doing around you, and how can you join Him?

_____
_____
_____

## Together Challenge:

Pray with someone today.

## Daily Reading:

Job 28:1-28, Psalm 111:1-10, Luke 5:17-32

## Study Journal Question:

1. How does Job and Psalm 111 describe wisdom?
2. How does Psalm 111 describe the works of the Lord?
3. Why does Jesus associate with sinners?
4. Would you be found among the tax collectors or Pharisees? Why?
5. How is God revealed in today's reading, and what does this mean for your life?

## Answers, Ponderings, and New Discoveries:

_____
_____
_____
_____
_____
_____
_____
_____
_____
_____
_____
_____

**Prayer Requests / Answers :** _____
_____
_____
_____

## What is God doing around you, and how can you join Him?

_____
_____
_____

## Together Challenge:

Share a meal with an unbeliever.

## Daily Reading:

Proverbs 1:1-33, Matthew 9:9-13, Mark 2:13-17

## Study Journal Question:

1. What happens to those who do not fear the Lord?
2. Why is wisdom valuable?
3. Why did Jesus say He desired mercy and not sacrifice?
4. How have you responded to Jesus' call to follow Him?
5. How is God revealed in today's reading, and what does this mean for your life?

## Answers, Ponderings, and New Discoveries:

_____
_____
_____
_____
_____
_____
_____
_____
_____
_____
_____
_____

**Prayer Requests / Answers :** _____
_____
_____
_____

## What is God doing around you, and how can you join Him?

_____
_____
_____

## Together Challenge:

Visit with someone you respect and ask them for words of wisdom.

## Daily Reading:

Job 29:1-25, Mark 2:18-22, Matthew 9:14-17, Luke 5:33-39

## Study Journal Question:

1. What was Job's life like before his trials?
2. Why didn't Jesus' disciples fast?
3. What was Jesus teaching in His parable?
4. Are you in a season of eating and drinking or fasting? Why?
5. How is God revealed in today's reading, and what does this mean for your life?

## Answers, Ponderings, and New Discoveries:

_____
_____
_____
_____
_____
_____
_____
_____
_____
_____
_____
_____

**Prayer Requests / Answers :** _____
_____
_____
_____

## What is God doing around you, and how can you join Him?

_____
_____
_____

## Together Challenge:

Celebrate or fast with someone today.

# Daily Reading:

Job 30:1-31, John 5:1-15

# Study Journal Question:

1. How did people treat Job after he lost everything?
2. What are the three instructions Jesus gave the invalid?
3. How would you describe the faith of the invalid?
4. When Jesus asks you if you want to be healed, how do you respond?
5. How is God revealed in today's reading, and what does this mean for your life?

# Answers, Ponderings, and New Discoveries:

_____
_____
_____
_____
_____
_____
_____
_____
_____
_____
_____

**Prayer Requests / Answers :** _____
_____
_____
_____

# What is God doing around you, and how can you join Him?

_____
_____
_____

# Together Challenge:

Encourage someone to turn away from sin.

## Daily Reading:

Psalm 9:1-20, Psalm 75:1-10, John 5:16-47

## Study Journal Question:

1. How does God judge the world?
2. How does the resurrection affect your understanding of God's justice?
3. How does Jesus describe the purpose of the scriptures?
4. Do you act like your judge is God or people? Why?
5. How is God revealed in today's reading, and what does this mean for your life?

## Answers, Ponderings, and New Discoveries:

_____
_____
_____
_____
_____
_____
_____
_____
_____
_____
_____
_____

**Prayer Requests / Answers :** _____
_____
_____
_____

## What is God doing around you, and how can you join Him?

_____
_____
_____

## Together Challenge:

Do not receive glory from others, but seek the glory that comes from the only God.

## Daily Reading:

Job 31:1-40

## Study Journal Question:

1. How can you follow Job's example of sexual purity?
2. Job referred to the good works in his life. What kind of works do you do?
3. How does Job condemn putting confidence in wealth?
4. From the list Job provides, what areas are you weak in, and what can you do to improve?
5. How is God revealed in today's reading, and what does this mean for your life?

## Answers, Ponderings, and New Discoveries:

_____
_____
_____
_____
_____
_____
_____
_____
_____
_____
_____

**Prayer Requests / Answers :** _____
_____
_____
_____

## What is God doing around you, and how can you join Him?

_____
_____
_____

## Together Challenge:

Talk with someone about where you are falling short.

## Daily Reading:

Job 32:1-22

## Study Journal Question:

1. Why was Elihu angry?
2. How did Elihu respect those who were older than him?
3. Who does Elihu identify as wise? Why?
4. Which of the 5 people who have spoken in the book of Job do you relate to the most? Why?
5. How is God revealed in today's reading, and what does this mean for your life?

## Answers, Ponderings, and New Discoveries:

_____
_____
_____
_____
_____
_____
_____
_____
_____
_____
_____

**Prayer Requests / Answers :** _____
_____
_____
_____

## What is God doing around you, and how can you join Him?

_____
_____
_____

## Together Challenge:

Listen before you speak in your conversations today.

## Daily Reading:

Job 33:1-33, Matthew 12:1-8

## Study Journal Question:

1. What does Elihu indicate that God uses to motivate people to repent?
2. What did Elihu say that Job had done wrong?
3. Why were the Pharisees upset?
4. How has your ignorance caused you to condemn the guiltless?
5. How is God revealed in today's reading, and what does this mean for your life?

## Answers, Ponderings, and New Discoveries:

_____
_____
_____
_____
_____
_____
_____
_____
_____
_____
_____

**Prayer Requests / Answers :** _____
_____
_____
_____

## What is God doing around you, and how can you join Him?

_____
_____
_____

## Together Challenge:

Listen to people first before judging their actions.

## Daily Reading:

Job 34:1-37, Luke 6:1-5, Mark 2:23-28

## Study Journal Question:

1. What does Elihu accuse Job of today?
2. How does Elihu defend God?
3. Why was the Sabbath given?
4. How does Jesus being Lord of the Sabbath affect us today?
5. How is God revealed in today's reading, and what does this mean for your life?

## Answers, Ponderings, and New Discoveries:

_____
_____
_____
_____
_____
_____
_____
_____
_____
_____
_____
_____

**Prayer Requests / Answers :** _____
_____
_____
_____

## What is God doing around you, and how can you join Him?

_____
_____
_____

## Together Challenge:

Stand up for what is true among those who have believed a lie.

## Daily Reading:

Job 35:1-36:21, Mark 3:1-6, Luke 6:6-11

## Study Journal Question:

1. According to Elihu, at what point does God not hear a man's cry?
2. How have you missed what God was doing in your life because you were expecting something else?
3. Why didn't the Pharisees believe Jesus?
4. How did Jesus silence the Pharisees?
5. How is God revealed in today's reading, and what does this mean for your life?

## Answers, Ponderings, and New Discoveries:

_____
_____
_____
_____
_____
_____
_____
_____
_____
_____
_____

**Prayer Requests / Answers :** _____
_____
_____

## What is God doing around you, and how can you join Him?

_____
_____
_____

## Together Challenge:

Do something good for someone today.

## Daily Reading:

Job 36:22-37:24, Matthew 12:9-21

## Study Journal Question:

1. How is God's power revealed through nature?
2. What is the significance of Isaiah referring to the Gentiles?
3. How did Jesus show the Pharisees they were hypocrites through His analogy?
4. How have you felt God's presence and power in His creation?
5. How is God revealed in today's reading, and what does this mean for your life?

## Answers, Ponderings, and New Discoveries:

_____
_____
_____
_____
_____
_____
_____
_____
_____
_____
_____
_____

**Prayer Requests / Answers :** _____
_____
_____
_____

## What is God doing around you, and how can you join Him?

_____
_____
_____

## Together Challenge:

Proclaim the truth to someone without quarreling.

## Daily Reading:

Job 38:1-41, Mark 3:7-19

## Study Journal Question:

1. What was God's accusation against Job?
2. How does God explain that His knowledge and understanding is superior to man?
3. What were the twelve given the authority to do?
4. How can acknowledging God's power in creation keep you from complaining in life?
5. How is God revealed in today's reading, and what does this mean for your life?

## Answers, Ponderings, and New Discoveries:

_____
_____
_____
_____
_____
_____
_____
_____
_____
_____
_____

**Prayer Requests / Answers :** _____
_____
_____
_____

## What is God doing around you, and how can you join Him?

_____
_____
_____

## Together Challenge:

Go for a walk outside with someone and talk about God's power over creation.

## Daily Reading:

Job 39:1-30

## Study Journal Question:

1. How is God's wisdom made known through the animals?
2. How is God's power made known through the animals?
3. What was God's purpose in creating animals?
4. What can you learn about God from the animals He created?
5. How is God revealed in today's reading, and what does this mean for your life?

## Answers, Ponderings, and New Discoveries:

_____
_____
_____
_____
_____
_____
_____
_____
_____
_____
_____
_____

**Prayer Requests / Answers :** _____
_____
_____
_____

## What is God doing around you, and how can you join Him?

_____
_____
_____

## Together Challenge:

Go to a zoo or farm and admire God's creation with a friend.

        www.BibleStudyTogether.com

## Daily Reading:

Job 40:1-24

## Study Journal Question:

1. Which of Job's friends accused Job of the same thing that God did?
2. How did Job respond to God?
3. What is God trying to help Job recognize?
4. What does the behemoth look like?
5. How is God revealed in today's reading, and what does this mean for your life?

## Answers, Ponderings, and New Discoveries:

_____
_____
_____
_____
_____
_____
_____
_____
_____
_____
_____
_____

**Prayer Requests / Answers :** _____
_____
_____
_____

## What is God doing around you, and how can you join Him?

_____
_____
_____

## Together Challenge:

Draw and share a picture of a behemoth with someone.

## Daily Reading:

Job 41:1-34, Psalm 42:1-11, Luke 6:12-26

## Study Journal Question:

1. What does it look like to thirst for God and His righteousness?
2. What can you learn from the psalmist about dealing with turmoil?
3. If you fear the leviathan, how much more should you fear God?
4. What was Jesus doing before He chose the Twelve?
5. How is God revealed in today's reading, and what does this mean for your life?

## Answers, Ponderings, and New Discoveries:

_____
_____
_____
_____
_____
_____
_____
_____
_____
_____
_____
_____

**Prayer Requests / Answers :** _____
_____
_____
_____

## What is God doing around you, and how can you join Him?

_____
_____
_____

## Together Challenge:

Spend time in prayer with someone who is making a big decision.

## Daily Reading:

Matthew 5:1-12, Psalm 37:1-40

## Study Journal Question:

1. What does the psalmist say will happen to the wicked?
2. What are the qualities of those who will inherit the land/earth?
3. How do we become righteous and obtain the desires of our heart?
4. Why would Jesus say that those who are persecuted are blessed?
5. How is God revealed in today's reading, and what does this mean for your life?

## Answers, Ponderings, and New Discoveries:

_____
_____
_____
_____
_____
_____
_____
_____
_____
_____
_____
_____

**Prayer Requests / Answers :** _____
_____
_____

## What is God doing around you, and how can you join Him?

_____
_____
_____

## Together Challenge:

Bless someone for something unexpected.

## Daily Reading:

Job 42:1-17, Matthew 5:13-26, Proverbs 6:1-5

## Study Journal Question:

1. If what Job said throughout this book was not perfect, what did he say that was right that his friends did not say?
2. What can we learn about the way God works in our lives through the story of Job?
3. How are you salt and light in the world around you?
4. How does your righteousness exceed that of the Scribes and Pharisees?
5. How is God revealed in today's reading, and what does this mean for your life?

## Answers, Ponderings, and New Discoveries:

_____
_____
_____
_____
_____
_____
_____
_____
_____
_____
_____

**Prayer Requests / Answers :** _____
_____
_____
_____

## What is God doing around you, and how can you join Him?

_____
_____
_____

## Together Challenge:

Quickly deal with any conflicts you have in a relationship.

    

## Daily Reading:

Exodus 1:1-2:10, Matthew 5:27-48

## Study Journal Question:

1. Why did Pharaoh fear the Israelites and order the midwives to kill the baby boys?
2. How did God save Moses?
3. Which of the topics from Matthew is most challenging to you?
4. How does God view lust?
5. How is God revealed in today's reading, and what does this mean for your life?

## Answers, Ponderings, and New Discoveries:

_____
_____
_____
_____
_____
_____
_____
_____
_____
_____
_____
_____

**Prayer Requests / Answers :** _____
_____
_____
_____

## What is God doing around you, and how can you join Him?

_____
_____
_____

## Together Challenge:

Do something loving toward an enemy or someone who treats you poorly.

## Daily Reading:

Exodus  2:11-3:22, Luke 6:27-36, Matthew 6:1-4

## Study Journal Question:

1. Why did Moses kill the Egyptian?
2. What is the significance of the name God designated for himself?
3. What does it mean to be merciful even as your Father in heaven is merciful?
4. What is in your heart when you give to the needy?
5. How is God revealed in today's reading, and what does this mean for your life?

## Answers, Ponderings, and New Discoveries:

_____
_____
_____
_____
_____
_____
_____
_____
_____
_____
_____
_____

**Prayer Requests / Answers :** _____
_____
_____
_____

## What is God doing around you, and how can you join Him?

_____
_____
_____

## Together Challenge:

Give to someone without expecting anything in return.

## Daily Reading:

Exodus 4:1-31

## Study Journal Question:

1. What was Moses' response to God?
2. How did God prepare Moses for the unbelief of the people?
3. How did Moses and Aaron work together to accomplish God's purposes?
4. In what ways can you relate to Moses' struggle to follow God's command?
5. How is God revealed in today's reading, and what does this mean for your life?

## Answers, Ponderings, and New Discoveries:

_____
_____
_____
_____
_____
_____
_____
_____
_____
_____
_____
_____
_____

**Prayer Requests / Answers :** _____
_____
_____
_____

## What is God doing around you, and how can you join Him?

_____
_____
_____

## Together Challenge:

Worship God with others for an answered prayer.

## Daily Reading:

Exodus 5:1-6:13

## Study Journal Question:

1. How would you describe the faith of Moses?
2. Why are the Israelites angry at Moses and Aaron?
3. What was Pharaoh's perspective of God?
4. Why do people doubt that God can use them in difficult situations?
5. How is God revealed in today's reading, and what does this mean for your life?

## Answers, Ponderings, and New Discoveries:

_____
_____
_____
_____
_____
_____
_____
_____
_____
_____
_____

**Prayer Requests / Answers :** _____
_____
_____
_____

## What is God doing around you, and how can you join Him?

_____
_____
_____

## Together Challenge:

Inspire faith in someone who is struggling with doubt.

# Daily Reading:

Exodus 6:14-30, Matthew 6:5-34, Psalm 147:1-20

# Study Journal Question:

1. Why can we be confident that God will provide for us?
2. What is your motive for doing good?
3. How do people in the church try to impress others today?
4. What does it mean for you to seek first the kingdom of God?
5. How is God revealed in today's reading, and what does this mean for your life?

# Answers, Ponderings, and New Discoveries:

_____
_____
_____
_____
_____
_____
_____
_____
_____
_____
_____
_____

**Prayer Requests / Answers :** _____
_____
_____
_____

# What is God doing around you, and how can you join Him?

_____
_____
_____

# Together Challenge:

Lay up treasure in heaven by secretly being a blessing to someone else.

## Daily Reading:

Exodus 7:1-25, Matthew 7:1-6, Luke 6:37-42

## Study Journal Question:

1. How did Pharaoh respond to the signs God had given to Moses?
2. What does it mean to have a hard heart?
3. Why is it important to remove the log out of your eye first?
4. How do you fare when you measure yourself by the standards you use to judge others?
5. How is God revealed in today's reading, and what does this mean for your life?

## Answers, Ponderings, and New Discoveries:

_____
_____
_____
_____
_____
_____
_____
_____
_____
_____
_____

**Prayer Requests / Answers :** _____
_____
_____
_____

## What is God doing around you, and how can you join Him?

_____
_____
_____

## Together Challenge:

Give to someone with the measure you like to receive.

## Daily Reading:

Exodus 8:1-19, Psalm 20:1-9, Matthew 7:7-20, Luke 6:43-45

## Study Journal Question:

1. How did Pharaoh respond to the plagues?
2. How does God respond to those who make requests of Him?
3. Based on the fruit in your life, what will happen to you in the end?
4. What does it mean to enter by the narrow gate?
5. How is God revealed in today's reading, and what does this mean for your life?

## Answers, Ponderings, and New Discoveries:

_____
_____
_____
_____
_____
_____
_____
_____
_____
_____
_____

**Prayer Requests / Answers :** _____
_____
_____

## What is God doing around you, and how can you join Him?

_____
_____
_____

## Together Challenge:

Encourage someone to not put their trust in the things of this world.

## Daily Reading:

Psalm 6:1-10, Proverbs 9:1-18, Exodus 8:20-32, Matthew 7:21-29

## Study Journal Question:

1. How is a person's wisdom determined by who they listen to?
2. Was Pharaoh building his house on the sand or the rock? Why?
3. How do wisdom and folly both cry out?
4. How can you do something in Jesus' name, but still reject the will of the Father?
5. How is God revealed in today's reading, and what does this mean for your life?

## Answers, Ponderings, and New Discoveries:

_____
_____
_____
_____
_____
_____
_____
_____
_____
_____
_____
_____

**Prayer Requests / Answers :** _____
_____
_____
_____

## What is God doing around you, and how can you join Him?

_____
_____
_____

## Together Challenge:

Pray with someone that God would make His power known to the hard-hearted.

## Daily Reading:

Psalm 50:1-23, Exodus 9:1-7, Luke 6:46-49, Matthew 8:5-13

## Study Journal Question:

1. Though God doesn't need anything, what does He want from us?
2. How did God make a distinction between the people of Israel and the Egyptians?
3. What can we learn from the Psalm and Luke about how God regards those who don't listen to Him?
4. How would you describe your faith?
5. How is God revealed in today's reading, and what does this mean for your life?

## Answers, Ponderings, and New Discoveries:

_____
_____
_____
_____
_____
_____
_____
_____
_____
_____
_____

**Prayer Requests / Answers :** _____
_____
_____

## What is God doing around you, and how can you join Him?

_____
_____
_____

## Together Challenge:

Talk with someone about the foundation you are building on.

## Daily Reading:

Exodus 9:8-35

## Study Journal Question:

1. Why did God exalt Pharaoh and not kill him?
2. What can we learn about the way God accomplishes His will by the way He deals with Pharaoh?
3. What was Pharaoh's initial response after the thunder and hail?
4. How have you responded when God brought trials into your life? Can you relate to Pharaoh?
5. How is God revealed in today's reading, and what does this mean for your life?

## Answers, Ponderings, and New Discoveries:

_____
_____
_____
_____
_____
_____
_____
_____
_____
_____
_____
_____

**Prayer Requests / Answers :** _____
_____
_____
_____

## What is God doing around you, and how can you join Him?

_____
_____
_____

## Together Challenge:

Share with someone about how God made His power known to you.

## Daily Reading:

Exodus 10:1-11:10

## Study Journal Question:

1. Why didn't Pharaoh want the Israelites to leave with everything?
2. How did Pharaoh's servants respond to the plagues?
3. What happened in Moses and Pharaoh's last interaction?
4. How have you responded when someone persistently refused your request?
5. How is God revealed in today's reading, and what does this mean for your life?

## Answers, Ponderings, and New Discoveries:

_____
_____
_____
_____
_____
_____
_____
_____
_____
_____
_____

**Prayer Requests / Answers :** _____
_____
_____

## What is God doing around you, and how can you join Him?

_____
_____
_____

## Together Challenge:

Continue to do what God has shown you even when God's enemies stand opposed to you.

## Daily Reading:

Exodus 12:1-30, Luke 7:1-17

## Study Journal Question:

1. What is the significance of the Passover, and why do Christians remember it today?
2. What would it be like if our nation experienced such a severe plague?
3. What made the centurion's faith great?
4. How have you experienced the Lord's compassion like the widow?
5. How is God revealed in today's reading, and what does this mean for your life?

## Answers, Ponderings, and New Discoveries:

_____
_____
_____
_____
_____
_____
_____
_____
_____
_____
_____
_____

**Prayer Requests / Answers :** _____
_____
_____
_____

## What is God doing around you, and how can you join Him?

_____
_____
_____

## Together Challenge:

Remind the people around you about the miracles that Jesus has done.

## Daily Reading:

Exodus 12:31-51, Matthew 11:1-19

## Study Journal Question:

1. What was Pharaoh's reaction to the last plague?
2. What rule was established for the stranger who sojourns among the Israelites?
3. Who was John the Baptist, and what was his role?
4. What can you do to become the greatest in the kingdom of heaven?
5. How is God revealed in today's reading, and what does this mean for your life?

## Answers, Ponderings, and New Discoveries:

_____
_____
_____
_____
_____
_____
_____
_____
_____
_____
_____
_____

**Prayer Requests / Answers :** _____
_____
_____
_____

## What is God doing around you, and how can you join Him?

_____
_____
_____

## Together Challenge:

Befriend someone who has been rejected by society.

     

## Daily Reading:

Exodus 13:1-14:4, Luke 7:18-35

## Study Journal Question:

1. What is similar about the way God led the Israelites and the way He leads you now?
2. Why did God command the people to eat unleavened bread?
3. Why did John send his disciples to Jesus?
4. What did Jesus mean when He said, "wisdom is justified by all her children"?
5. How is God revealed in today's reading, and what does this mean for your life?

## Answers, Ponderings, and New Discoveries:

_____
_____
_____
_____
_____
_____
_____
_____
_____
_____
_____

**Prayer Requests / Answers :** _____

_____
_____
_____

## What is God doing around you, and how can you join Him?

_____
_____
_____

## Together Challenge:

Do something special with others to remember what God has done for you.

## Daily Reading:

Exodus 14:5-31, Matthew 11:20-30

## Study Journal Question:

1. How did Moses work great miracles?
2. How did God deliver the Israelites?
3. How does Jesus being gentle and humble in heart change the way you see Him denouncing people?
4. What can we learn about God's character from the way He interacted with the Israelites?
5. How is God revealed in today's reading, and what does this mean for your life?

## Answers, Ponderings, and New Discoveries:

_____
_____
_____
_____
_____
_____
_____
_____
_____
_____
_____

**Prayer Requests / Answers :** _____
_____
_____
_____

## What is God doing around you, and how can you join Him?

_____
_____
_____

## Together Challenge:

Inspire someone who is doubting to follow God's leading.

## Daily Reading:

Exodus 15:1-27, Luke 7:36-50

## Study Journal Question:

1. How did the Israelites respond to God's deliverance?
2. What did God promise the Israelites if they kept His statutes?
3. How did Jesus' response to the woman differ from the Pharisees?
4. How has the way you have been forgiven affect the way you love God and others?
5. How is God revealed in today's reading, and what does this mean for your life?

## Answers, Ponderings, and New Discoveries:

_____
_____
_____
_____
_____
_____
_____
_____
_____
_____
_____

**Prayer Requests / Answers :** _____
_____
_____
_____

## What is God doing around you, and how can you join Him?

_____
_____
_____

## Together Challenge:

Share with someone how you have been forgiven.

## Daily Reading:

Exodus 16:1-36

## Study Journal Question:

1. How did God test the people of Israel?
2. Which actions of the Israelites indicate their level of faith?
3. How did the people treat Moses and Aaron?
4. In what ways are you daily dependent on God like the Israelites?
5. How is God revealed in today's reading, and what does this mean for your life?

## Answers, Ponderings, and New Discoveries:

_____
_____
_____
_____
_____
_____
_____
_____
_____
_____
_____

**Prayer Requests / Answers :** _____
_____
_____
_____

## What is God doing around you, and how can you join Him?

_____
_____
_____

## Together Challenge:

Measure out 9.3 cups (an omer) of oatmeal with someone and see how much mana an Israelite gathered for each day.

## Daily Reading:

Exodus 17:1-18:27

## Study Journal Question:

1. How did the Israelites respond to difficulty?
2. Why will God war against the Amalekites?
3. What did Moses learn from his father-in-law?
4. What valuable life lesson have you learned from your parents?
5. How is God revealed in today's reading, and what does this mean for your life?

## Answers, Ponderings, and New Discoveries:

_____
_____
_____
_____
_____
_____
_____
_____
_____
_____
_____

**Prayer Requests / Answers :** _____
_____
_____
_____

## What is God doing around you, and how can you join Him?

_____
_____
_____

## Together Challenge:

Find other people to work together in fulfilling God's calling.

## Daily Reading:

Exodus 19:1-25, Luke 8:1-3, Mark 3:20-30

## Study Journal Question:

1. What was God's intent for the nation of Israel?
2. Why couldn't the people of Israel go up the mountain?
3. What was Jesus' defense against the accusation that he was possessed by Satan?
4. What has changed about the way you are able to approach God compared to the people of Israel?
5. How is God revealed in today's reading, and what does this mean for your life?

## Answers, Ponderings, and New Discoveries:

_____
_____
_____
_____
_____
_____
_____
_____
_____
_____

**Prayer Requests / Answers :** _____
_____
_____
_____

## What is God doing around you, and how can you join Him?

_____
_____
_____

## Together Challenge:

Encourage those who are ill and broken to follow Jesus.

## Daily Reading:

Exodus 20:1-26, Matthew 12:22-45

## Study Journal Question:

1. How will you be judged based on your words?
2. How does God respond to those who speak against Him and use His name in vain?
3. Why did God want the Israelites to fear Him?
4. Why will the men of Nineveh and the queen of the South condemn people?
5. How is God revealed in today's reading, and what does this mean for your life?

## Answers, Ponderings, and New Discoveries:

_____
_____
_____
_____
_____
_____
_____
_____
_____
_____
_____
_____

**Prayer Requests / Answers :** _____
_____
_____
_____

## What is God doing around you, and how can you join Him?

_____
_____
_____

## Together Challenge:

Find some way to honor your father and mother.

## Daily Reading:

Exodus 21:1-36, Matthew 12:46-50, Mark 3:31-35

## Study Journal Question:

1. What was God trying to teach the people by giving the laws found in today's reading?
2. Why do the laws have various levels of consequences?
3. Why does Jesus consider those who do the will of God to be His family?
4. Who do you consider to be your brother, sister, and mother?
5. How is God revealed in today's reading, and what does this mean for your life?

## Answers, Ponderings, and New Discoveries:

_____
_____
_____
_____
_____
_____
_____
_____
_____
_____
_____
_____

**Prayer Requests / Answers :** _____
_____
_____
_____

## What is God doing around you, and how can you join Him?

_____
_____
_____

## Together Challenge:

Spend some time with your spiritual family today.

## Daily Reading:

Exodus 22:1-31, Luke 8:19-21, Mark 4:1-9

## Study Journal Question:

1. How does the law teach us to treat those who borrow from us?
2. What can we see about God's heart in the Law concerning the fatherless and widows?
3. What is the significance of hearing in Mark and Luke?
4. What can you apply from the Law to your life about how to treat your neighbor?
5. How is God revealed in today's reading, and what does this mean for your life?

## Answers, Ponderings, and New Discoveries:

_____
_____
_____
_____
_____
_____
_____
_____
_____
_____
_____
_____

**Prayer Requests / Answers :** _____
_____
_____
_____

## What is God doing around you, and how can you join Him?

_____
_____
_____

## Together Challenge:

If you have damaged someone's property, do what it takes to make things right.

    

## Daily Reading:

Exodus 23:1-33, Luke 8:4-8, Matthew 13:1-9

## Study Journal Question:

1. What does the law teach us about honesty?
2. How did God plan to guide the Israelites into the land?
3. How did the people respond to Jesus' Ministry?
4. What area of your life produces the most fruit?
5. How is God revealed in today's reading, and what does this mean for your life?

## Answers, Ponderings, and New Discoveries:

_____
_____
_____
_____
_____
_____
_____
_____
_____
_____
_____

**Prayer Requests / Answers :** _____
_____
_____
_____

## What is God doing around you, and how can you join Him?

_____
_____
_____

## Together Challenge:

Treat a foreigner with kindness.

## Daily Reading:

Exodus 24:1-25:9

## Study Journal Question:

1. Why did Moses put blood on people and things?
2. How did the Israelites respond to the commands of God in today's reading?
3. What was God's instruction to Moses concerning the building of the Tabernacle?
4. How would you respond if you were one of the elders on the mountain?
5. How is God revealed in today's reading, and what does this mean for your life?

## Answers, Ponderings, and New Discoveries:

_____
_____
_____
_____
_____
_____
_____
_____
_____
_____
_____
_____

**Prayer Requests / Answers :** _____
_____
_____
_____

## What is God doing around you, and how can you join Him?

_____
_____
_____

## Together Challenge:

Contribute something to collectively accomplish the work of the Lord.

## Daily Reading:

Exodus 25:10-40

## Study Journal Question:

1. What is the significance of the material used in building the Tabernacle furnishings?
2. Why was God so specific about how to build things?
3. Where did God decide to meet with the people?
4. How has God given you very specific instructions in your life?
5. How is God revealed in today's reading, and what does this mean for your life?

## Answers, Ponderings, and New Discoveries:

_____
_____
_____
_____
_____
_____
_____
_____
_____
_____
_____

**Prayer Requests / Answers :** _____
_____
_____
_____

## What is God doing around you, and how can you join Him?

_____
_____
_____

## Together Challenge:

Draw either the Ark of the Covenant or the lamp stand and show it to someone.

## Daily Reading:

Exodus 26:1-37, Matthew 13:10-23

## Study Journal Question:

1. What was the quality of the materials used to make the Tabernacle?
2. Why did Jesus speak in parables?
3. Which soil describes the way you hear?
4. Why were Jesus disciples able to see and hear?
5. How is God revealed in today's reading, and what does this mean for your life?

## Answers, Ponderings, and New Discoveries:

_____
_____
_____
_____
_____
_____
_____
_____
_____
_____
_____
_____

**Prayer Requests / Answers :** _____
_____
_____
_____

## What is God doing around you, and how can you join Him?

_____
_____
_____

## Together Challenge:

Help someone to hear and understand God's word.

## Daily Reading:

Exodus 27:1-28:5, Mark 4:10-20

## Study Journal Question:

1. Who did God choose to be priests?
2. How is this parable the key to understanding other parables?
3. What rocks and thorns are in your life?
4. What do you need to make your soil good and able to receive the word of God?
5. How is God revealed in today's reading, and what does this mean for your life?

## Answers, Ponderings, and New Discoveries:

_____
_____
_____
_____
_____
_____
_____
_____
_____
_____
_____

**Prayer Requests / Answers :** _____
_____
_____

## What is God doing around you, and how can you join Him?

_____
_____
_____

## Together Challenge:

Talk with someone about the kind of soil your heart is made of.

## Daily Reading:

Exodus 28:6-43, Luke 8:9-18

## Study Journal Question:

1. Why did Jesus only explain the parable to His disciples?
2. What does the seed represent and how does the devil take it away?
3. What was the significance of engraving the names of tribes of Israel on the stones?
4. How can you prevent what you have from being taken away?
5. How is God revealed in today's reading, and what does this mean for your life?

## Answers, Ponderings, and New Discoveries:

_____
_____
_____
_____
_____
_____
_____
_____
_____
_____
_____
_____
_____

**Prayer Requests / Answers :** _____

_____
_____
_____

## What is God doing around you, and how can you join Him?

_____
_____
_____

## Together Challenge:

Help someone understand and receive the word of God.

## Daily Reading:

Exodus 29:1-46, 2 Corinthians 1:1-11

## Study Journal Question:

1. Why does God ask the people to sacrifice?
2. What purpose does the tent of meeting serve for the people of Israel?
3. What is the purpose of suffering?
4. How have you been comforted?
5. How is God revealed in today's reading, and what does this mean for your life?

## Answers, Ponderings, and New Discoveries:

_____
_____
_____
_____
_____
_____
_____
_____
_____
_____
_____
_____

**Prayer Requests / Answers :** _____

_____
_____
_____

## What is God doing around you, and how can you join Him?

_____
_____
_____

## Together Challenge:

Encourage someone who's facing a similar trial that you have faced.

## Daily Reading:

Exodus 30:1-33, 2 Corinthians 1:12–2:4

## Study Journal Question:

1. What does it mean for the Tabernacle and its accessories to be holy?
2. What did God ask Moses to do along with the census?
3. What does it mean for the promises of God to find their "yes" in Jesus Christ?
4. Paul boasted about certain things. What do you boast about?
5. How is God revealed in today's reading, and what does this mean for your life?

## Answers, Ponderings, and New Discoveries:

_____
_____
_____
_____
_____
_____
_____
_____
_____
_____
_____
_____

**Prayer Requests / Answers :** _____
_____
_____
_____

## What is God doing around you, and how can you join Him?

_____
_____
_____

## Together Challenge:

Write a letter to someone to express your care for them.

## Daily Reading:

Exodus 30:34-31:18

## Study Journal Question:

1. How did God equip the people to build the Tabernacle?
2. How has God equipped you to serve Him?
3. What sign did the Sabbath symbolize and to whom was it given?
4. How was the blend of incense to be used?
5. How is God revealed in today's reading, and what does this mean for your life?

## Answers, Ponderings, and New Discoveries:

_____
_____
_____
_____
_____
_____
_____
_____
_____
_____
_____

**Prayer Requests / Answers :** _____
_____
_____
_____

## What is God doing around you, and how can you join Him?

_____
_____
_____

## Together Challenge:

Rest and be refreshed with others today.

## Daily Reading:

Exodus 32:1-35

## Study Journal Question:

1. Why did the people worship a false god?
2. How did Moses respond to the people's sin?
3. How did God respond to the people's sin?
4. Who can you pray for like Moses prayed for the Israelites?
5. How is God revealed in today's reading, and what does this mean for your life?

## Answers, Ponderings, and New Discoveries:

_____
_____
_____
_____
_____
_____
_____
_____
_____
_____
_____
_____

**Prayer Requests / Answers :** _____
_____
_____
_____

## What is God doing around you, and how can you join Him?

_____
_____
_____

## Together Challenge:

Actively wait on God with your family and your church.

        

## Daily Reading:

Exodus 33:1-23, 2 Corinthians 2:5-3:6

## Study Journal Question:

1. What is the purpose of the tent of meeting?
2. Why was Moses concerned about God's presence going with them?
3. Why are Christians both the fragrance of life and death?
4. How have you experienced both the effects of the letter and the spirit?
5. How is God revealed in today's reading, and what does this mean for your life?

## Answers, Ponderings, and New Discoveries:

_____
_____
_____
_____
_____
_____
_____
_____
_____
_____
_____

**Prayer Requests / Answers :** _____
_____
_____

## What is God doing around you, and how can you join Him?

_____
_____
_____

## Together Challenge:

Reaffirm your love for someone who has caused you grief or pain.

## Daily Reading:

Exodus 34:1-35:3, 2 Corinthians 3:7-18

## Study Journal Question:

1. How does God describe himself?
2. How does the Covenant that was given to Moses differ from the Covenant that came through Jesus Christ?
3. What does the veil on Moses' face symbolize?
4. How have you been transformed by having an unveiled face?
5. How is God revealed in today's reading, and what does this mean for your life?

## Answers, Ponderings, and New Discoveries:

_____
_____
_____
_____
_____
_____
_____
_____
_____
_____
_____

**Prayer Requests / Answers :** _____
_____
_____
_____

## What is God doing around you, and how can you join Him?

_____
_____
_____

## Together Challenge:

Talk with others about the hope and freedom that is found and serving the one true God.

## Daily Reading:

Exodus 35:4-29, 2 Corinthians 4:1-18, Psalm 116:1-19

## Study Journal Question:

1. What type of people contributed toward the Tabernacle?
2. How have you come to know the glory of God?
3. What does it mean to fix our eyes on what is unseen?
4. Why does God put His treasure in jars of clay?
5. How is God revealed in today's reading, and what does this mean for your life?

## Answers, Ponderings, and New Discoveries:

_____
_____
_____
_____
_____
_____
_____
_____
_____
_____
_____
_____

**Prayer Requests / Answers :** _____
_____
_____
_____

## What is God doing around you, and how can you join Him?

_____
_____
_____

## Together Challenge:

What you believe, speak to someone else.

## Daily Reading:

Exodus 35:30-36:7, 2 Corinthians 5:1-6:2, Psalm 130:1-8

## Study Journal Question:

1. What does it mean to wait for the Lord?
2. What does it mean to be a New Creation?
3. Why does Paul fear the Lord?
4. How does the truth that Christ died for you impact the way you live?
5. How is God revealed in today's reading, and what does this mean for your life?

## Answers, Ponderings, and New Discoveries:

_____
_____
_____
_____
_____
_____
_____
_____
_____
_____
_____
_____

**Prayer Requests / Answers :** _____
_____
_____
_____

## What is God doing around you, and how can you join Him?

_____
_____
_____

## Together Challenge:

Generously give to the work of the Lord.

## Daily Reading:

Exodus 36:8-38, 2 Corinthians 6:3-7:1

## Study Journal Question:

1. How are the people responding to God's specific instructions about how to build the Tabernacle?
2. What is different about how God dwelt among the people of Israel versus how he dwells among us today?
3. What does it mean to be unequally yoked?
4. How does Paul's ministry as a servant of God compare to the way you serve God?
5. How is God revealed in today's reading, and what does this mean for your life?

## Answers, Ponderings, and New Discoveries:

_____
_____
_____
_____
_____
_____
_____
_____
_____
_____

**Prayer Requests / Answers :** _____
_____
_____
_____

## What is God doing around you, and how can you join Him?

_____
_____
_____

## Together Challenge:

Talk with someone about what it means to not touch the unclean things.

## Daily Reading:

Exodus 37:1-29

## Study Journal Question:

1. Where did God instruct Moses to place the furnishings in today's reading?
2. What was the purpose of the Ark of the Covenant?
3. How were the furnishings in today's reading supposed to be transported?
4. Compare the quality and precision used in building the Tabernacle to the way that you build your spiritual life?
5. How is God revealed in today's reading, and what does this mean for your life?

## Answers, Ponderings, and New Discoveries:

_____
_____
_____
_____
_____
_____
_____
_____
_____
_____
_____
_____

**Prayer Requests / Answers :** _____
_____
_____
_____

## What is God doing around you, and how can you join Him?

_____
_____
_____

## Together Challenge:

Ask a wise person how they build their relationship with God.

## Daily Reading:

Exodus 38:1-31

## Study Journal Question:

1. Who oversaw the building of the Tabernacle?
2. What was made out of bronze, and what was made out of silver?
3. Why is there a specific description of what the people made?
4. How does God call you to work with others to accomplish His will?
5. How is God revealed in today's reading, and what does this mean for your life?

## Answers, Ponderings, and New Discoveries:

_____
_____
_____
_____
_____
_____
_____
_____
_____
_____
_____
_____

**Prayer Requests / Answers :** _____
_____
_____
_____

## What is God doing around you, and how can you join Him?

_____
_____
_____

## Together Challenge:

Use your God-given gifts to bless your neighbor today.

## Daily Reading:

Exodus 39:1-7, 2 Corinthians 7:2-16, Psalm 38:1-22

## Study Journal Question:

1. What is the difference between Godly grief and worldly grief?
2. How does today's Psalm describe Godly sorrow and grief?
3. What comforted Paul?
4. How has God comforted you through another person?
5. How is God revealed in today's reading, and what does this mean for your life?

## Answers, Ponderings, and New Discoveries:

_____
_____
_____
_____
_____
_____
_____
_____
_____
_____
_____
_____

**Prayer Requests / Answers :** _____
_____
_____
_____

## What is God doing around you, and how can you join Him?

_____
_____
_____

## Together Challenge:

Make room in your heart for others.

## Daily Reading:

Exodus 39:8-43, Mark 4:21-29

## Study Journal Question:

1. Whose instruction did the people of Israel follow when they built the Tabernacle?
2. How did Moses respond when the Tabernacle was completed?
3. What is growing in your life as a result of the seeds that have been scattered?
4. Why will God take things away from those who already lack?
5. How is God revealed in today's reading, and what does this mean for your life?

## Answers, Ponderings, and New Discoveries:

_____
_____
_____
_____
_____
_____
_____
_____
_____
_____
_____
_____

**Prayer Requests / Answers :** _____
_____
_____
_____

## What is God doing around you, and how can you join Him?

_____
_____
_____

## Together Challenge:

Encourage someone to do the work that God has called them to do.

## Daily Reading:

Exodus 40:1-38, Mark 4:30-34, Matthew 13:24-30

## Study Journal Question:

1. What is the significance of the cloud?
2. How is the mustard seed like the kingdom of God?
3. What do the weeds symbolize, and how will the master get rid of them?
4. If today was harvest day, would you be in the barn or in the bundles?
5. How is God revealed in today's reading, and what does this mean for your life?

## Answers, Ponderings, and New Discoveries:

_____
_____
_____
_____
_____
_____
_____
_____
_____
_____
_____
_____

**Prayer Requests / Answers :** _____
_____
_____
_____

## What is God doing around you, and how can you join Him?

_____
_____
_____

## Together Challenge:

Explain the parable to someone who has ears to hear.

## Daily Reading:

Psalm 78:1-39, Matthew 13:31-52

## Study Journal Question:

1. Why should you teach the next generation about the works of the Lord?
2. How did God respond to the Israelites when they were not faithful to His covenant?
3. What will ultimately happen to the evil and the lawbreakers?
4. What significance do parables have?
5. How is God revealed in today's reading, and what does this mean for your life?

## Answers, Ponderings, and New Discoveries:

_____
_____
_____
_____
_____
_____
_____
_____
_____
_____
_____
_____

**Prayer Requests / Answers :** _____
_____
_____
_____

## What is God doing around you, and how can you join Him?

_____
_____
_____

## Together Challenge:

Share with someone a parable about the kingdom of heaven.

## Daily Reading:

Psalm 78:40-72, Mark 4:35-41, Matthew 8:23-27, Luke 8:22-25

## Study Journal Question:

1. Why did the psalmist write that the Israelites tested God again and again?
2. Why did the Disciples awake Jesus?
3. How would Jesus describe your faith?
4. How was God's power displayed to the disciples?
5. How is God revealed in today's reading, and what does this mean for your life?

## Answers, Ponderings, and New Discoveries:

_____
_____
_____
_____
_____
_____
_____
_____
_____
_____
_____
_____

**Prayer Requests / Answers :** _____
_____
_____
_____

## What is God doing around you, and how can you join Him?

_____
_____
_____

## Together Challenge:

Remind someone about God's power over the weather.

## Daily Reading:

Numbers 7:1-35

## Study Journal Question:

1. Why did God give the Levites the wagons and the oxen?
2. Why were the sons of Kohath not given wagons?
3. Why were the Chiefs bringing offerings?
4. What do you give as an offering to the Lord?
5. How is God revealed in today's reading, and what does this mean for your life?

## Answers, Ponderings, and New Discoveries:

_____
_____
_____
_____
_____
_____
_____
_____
_____
_____
_____
_____

**Prayer Requests / Answers :** _____
_____
_____
_____

## What is God doing around you, and how can you join Him?

_____
_____
_____

## Together Challenge:

Give a gift to a person that will help in their service to the Lord.

     www.BibleStudyTogether.com

## Daily Reading:

Numbers 7:36-59, Numbers 9:15-23

## Study Journal Question:

1. How did God command the Israelites to camp and set out?
2. What can you learn about God's leading from how long the Israelites camped at each location?
3. Which name of the leaders is the most fun to pronounce?
4. What is the cloud and fire in your life?
5. How is God revealed in today's reading, and what does this mean for your life?

## Answers, Ponderings, and New Discoveries:

_____
_____
_____
_____
_____
_____
_____
_____
_____
_____
_____
_____

**Prayer Requests / Answers :** _____
_____
_____
_____

## What is God doing around you, and how can you join Him?

_____
_____
_____

## Together Challenge:

Talk with someone about how God is leading you.

     

## Daily Reading:

Psalm 2:1-12, Psalm 45:1-17, Psalm 97:1-12, Hebrews 1:1-14

## Study Journal Question:

1. How is Jesus greater than the angels?
2. Why did God exalt Jesus?
3. How is God communicating with us throughout the ages?
4. How does God's righteousness rule and lay the foundation for your life?
5. How is God revealed in today's reading, and what does this mean for your life?

## Answers, Ponderings, and New Discoveries:

_____
_____
_____
_____
_____
_____
_____
_____
_____
_____
_____

**Prayer Requests / Answers :** _____
_____
_____

## What is God doing around you, and how can you join Him?

_____
_____
_____

## Together Challenge:

Rejoice in the Lord with someone else that God has made righteous.

## Daily Reading:

Psalm 104:1-35, Hebrews 2:1-18

## Study Journal Question:

1. How is God's wisdom made known through His works?
2. Why does the psalmist bless the Lord?
3. Why did Jesus have to be made like His brothers?
4. What causes you to drift and slip away?
5. How is God revealed in today's reading, and what does this mean for your life?

## Answers, Ponderings, and New Discoveries:

_____
_____
_____
_____
_____
_____
_____
_____
_____
_____
_____
_____

**Prayer Requests / Answers :** _____
_____
_____
_____

## What is God doing around you, and how can you join Him?

_____
_____
_____

## Together Challenge:

Sing God's praise in the midst of the congregation.

## Daily Reading:

Numbers 7:60-77, Psalm 95:1-11, Hebrews 3:1-19

## Study Journal Question:

1. How are we instructed to learn from the Israelites in the wilderness?
2. How does the psalmist teach us to respond to God?
3. Why couldn't the people enter God's rest?
4. Why is it important for you to hold fast to your confidence and hope?
5. How is God revealed in today's reading, and what does this mean for your life?

## Answers, Ponderings, and New Discoveries:

_____
_____
_____
_____
_____
_____
_____
_____
_____
_____
_____
_____

**Prayer Requests / Answers :** _____
_____
_____
_____

## What is God doing around you, and how can you join Him?

_____
_____
_____

## Together Challenge:

Exhort someone so they don't get hardened by sin.

## Daily Reading:

Psalm 29:1-11, Numbers 7:78-89, Hebrews 4:1-13

## Study Journal Question:

1. What is God's rest?
2. How do we enter rest?
3. What is God's voice like?
4. How has God's word impacted you?
5. How is God revealed in today's reading, and what does this mean for your life?

## Answers, Ponderings, and New Discoveries:

_____
_____
_____
_____
_____
_____
_____
_____
_____
_____
_____

**Prayer Requests / Answers :** _____
_____
_____
_____

## What is God doing around you, and how can you join Him?

_____
_____
_____

## Together Challenge:

Help someone find rest in God.

           

## Daily Reading:

Leviticus 8:1-36, Hebrews 4:14–5:10

## Study Journal Question:

1. Why can we confidently draw near to the throne of grace?
2. What was needed to be done for Aaron and his sons to serve as priests?
3. How is Jesus' priesthood superior to Aaron's?
4. How can Jesus sympathize with your weaknesses?
5. How is God revealed in today's reading, and what does this mean for your life?

## Answers, Ponderings, and New Discoveries:

_____
_____
_____
_____
_____
_____
_____
_____
_____
_____
_____
_____
_____

**Prayer Requests / Answers :** _____
_____
_____
_____

## What is God doing around you, and how can you join Him?

_____
_____
_____

## Together Challenge:

Share with someone why Jesus is the source of their salvation.

## Daily Reading:

Numbers 8:1-26

## Study Journal Question:

1. Why were the Levites set apart?
2. What did the Levites need to do to serve?
3. What special service did God appoint for the Levites?
4. How have you been dedicated to the Lord?
5. How is God revealed in today's reading, and what does this mean for your life?

## Answers, Ponderings, and New Discoveries:

_____
_____
_____
_____
_____
_____
_____
_____
_____
_____
_____
_____

**Prayer Requests / Answers :** _____

_____
_____
_____

## What is God doing around you, and how can you join Him?

_____
_____
_____

## Together Challenge:

Choose a particular service to perform for the Lord with your family members.

## Daily Reading:

Leviticus 9:1-24, Numbers 9:1-14

## Study Journal Question:

1. What offerings were performed for Aaron and the people?
2. Why did Aaron offer sacrifices on behalf of himself?
3. Who was supposed to keep the Passover?
4. How has God made provision for you when you are on a journey?
5. How is God revealed in today's reading, and what does this mean for your life?

## Answers, Ponderings, and New Discoveries:

_____
_____
_____
_____
_____
_____
_____
_____
_____
_____
_____
_____

**Prayer Requests / Answers :** _____
_____
_____
_____

## What is God doing around you, and how can you join Him?

_____
_____
_____

## Together Challenge:

Share with someone how God has appeared to you in a mighty way.

## Daily Reading:

Leviticus 10:1-20, Leviticus 5:14-19, Hebrews 5:11–6:12

## Study Journal Question:

1. How did Nadab and Abihu taste the heavenly gift and yet end up being burned?
2. Why were Ithamar and Eleazar forgiven?
3. How do Christians become dull of hearing?
4. What kind of crop are you bearing? Why?
5. How is God revealed in today's reading, and what does this mean for your life?

## Answers, Ponderings, and New Discoveries:

_____
_____
_____
_____
_____
_____
_____
_____
_____
_____
_____
_____

**Prayer Requests / Answers :** _____
_____
_____
_____

## What is God doing around you, and how can you join Him?

_____
_____
_____

## Together Challenge:

Show your love for Christ through serving the saints.

## Daily Reading:

Leviticus 2:1-16, Leviticus 5:1-13, Hebrews 6:13-20

## Study Journal Question:

1. Why is God's oath never rash?
2. Why do we not need to offer all the sacrifices the Israelites did for their sins?
3. What quality of offerings were the Israelites required to bring?
4. How is your hope an anchor of the soul?
5. How is God revealed in today's reading, and what does this mean for your life?

## Answers, Ponderings, and New Discoveries:

_____
_____
_____
_____
_____
_____
_____
_____
_____
_____
_____
_____

**Prayer Requests / Answers :** _____
_____
_____
_____

## What is God doing around you, and how can you join Him?

_____
_____
_____

## Together Challenge:

Encourage someone to hold fast to the hope set before them.

## Daily Reading:

Numbers 18:1-32, Hebrews 7:1-14

## Study Journal Question:

1. How did God provide for the Levites and the priests?
2. What is the significance of Jesus being a priest after the order of Melchizedek?
3. How do tithes apply to you today?
4. Why is there a change of the law for us today?
5. How is God revealed in today's reading, and what does this mean for your life?

## Answers, Ponderings, and New Discoveries:

_____
_____
_____
_____
_____
_____
_____
_____
_____
_____
_____

**Prayer Requests / Answers :** _____
_____
_____

## What is God doing around you, and how can you join Him?

_____
_____
_____

## Together Challenge:

Support those who minister to your spiritual needs.

## Daily Reading:

Jeremiah 30:1-24, Hebrews 7:15-28

## Study Journal Question:

1. How has God raised up David in the latter days?
2. How is Jesus different from other priests?
3. What gives you assurance that Jesus can completely save you?
4. How is our hope superior to the commandments of the law?
5. How is God revealed in today's reading, and what does this mean for your life?

## Answers, Ponderings, and New Discoveries:

_____
_____
_____
_____
_____
_____
_____
_____
_____
_____
_____

**Prayer Requests / Answers :** _____
_____
_____
_____

## What is God doing around you, and how can you join Him?

_____
_____
_____

## Together Challenge:

Remind the hopeless of the hope that Jesus brought.

## Daily Reading:

Jeremiah 31:1-40, Hebrews 8:1-13

## Study Journal Question:

1. What did God promise the nation of Israel?
2. What is the New Covenant?
3. How is the Old Covenant affected by the New Covenant?
4. How has God shown you mercy and forgiveness?
5. How is God revealed in today's reading, and what does this mean for your life?

## Answers, Ponderings, and New Discoveries:

_____
_____
_____
_____
_____
_____
_____
_____
_____
_____
_____
_____

**Prayer Requests / Answers :** _____
_____
_____
_____

## What is God doing around you, and how can you join Him?

_____
_____
_____

## Together Challenge:

Set up markers and guideposts for those who follow behind you.

## Daily Reading:
Numbers 19:1-22

## Study Journal Question:

1. How do unclean people become clean?
2. What happens to an unclean person if they do not cleanse themself?
3. How can uncleanness be spread?
4. In what ways have you experienced the cleansing power of Jesus?
5. How is God revealed in today's reading, and what does this mean for your life?

## Answers, Ponderings, and New Discoveries:

_____
_____
_____
_____
_____
_____
_____
_____
_____
_____
_____
_____

**Prayer Requests / Answers :** _____
_____
_____
_____

## What is God doing around you, and how can you join Him?
_____
_____
_____

## Together Challenge:

Encourage someone to stay morally pure.

## Daily Reading:

Leviticus 3:1-17, Leviticus 22:17-33

## Study Journal Question:

1. What was not acceptable to offer to the Lord?
2. What are the different kinds of sacrifices that the Israelites made?
3. What kind of sacrifices do you make to the Lord?
4. What were the Israelites commanded not to eat? Why?
5. How is God revealed in today's reading, and what does this mean for your life?

## Answers, Ponderings, and New Discoveries:

_____
_____
_____
_____
_____
_____
_____
_____
_____
_____
_____
_____

**Prayer Requests / Answers :** _____
_____
_____
_____

## What is God doing around you, and how can you join Him?

_____
_____
_____

## Together Challenge:

Grill some meat and smell a pleasing aroma with your friends.

## Daily Reading:
Leviticus 16:1-34, Hebrews 9:1-14

## Study Journal Question:

1. Why does Aaron need to make atonement for the Holy Place?
2. What was represented by the goat that was let go of the wilderness?
3. How did Jesus fulfill the sacrifice described in Leviticus?
4. How have you been impacted by what Jesus accomplished?
5. How is God revealed in today's reading, and what does this mean for your life?

## Answers, Ponderings, and New Discoveries:

_____
_____
_____
_____
_____
_____
_____
_____
_____
_____
_____

**Prayer Requests / Answers :** _____
_____
_____
_____

## What is God doing around you, and how can you join Him?

_____
_____
_____

## Together Challenge:

Share with someone how Jesus' sacrifice many years ago affects them today.

## Daily Reading:

Leviticus 6:1-30, Hebrews 9:15-28

## Study Journal Question:

1. What is the significance of the shedding of blood?
2. What made Jesus' sacrifice superior to the levitical priests' sacrifice?
3. How do you know if you will be saved when Jesus appears the second time?
4. What was required of Aaron and his sons when working with the Holy sacrifices?
5. How is God revealed in today's reading, and what does this mean for your life?

## Answers, Ponderings, and New Discoveries:

_____
_____
_____
_____
_____
_____
_____
_____
_____
_____
_____

**Prayer Requests / Answers :** _____
_____
_____
_____

## What is God doing around you, and how can you join Him?

_____
_____
_____

## Together Challenge:

Use the sacrificial system to help someone understand how their sins can be forgiven.

## Daily Reading:

Leviticus 1:1-17, Hebrews 10:1-18, Psalm 40:1-17

## Study Journal Question:

1. Why does God no longer require animal sacrifices?
2. How was the law a shadow of things to come?
3. How has God brought you out of the pit?
4. What does it mean for God to write His law on our hearts?
5. How is God revealed in today's reading, and what does this mean for your life?

## Answers, Ponderings, and New Discoveries:

_____
_____
_____
_____
_____
_____
_____
_____
_____
_____
_____
_____

**Prayer Requests / Answers :** _____
_____
_____
_____

## What is God doing around you, and how can you join Him?

_____
_____
_____

## Together Challenge:

Tell others about God's wondrous deeds.

## Daily Reading:

Leviticus 20:1-27, Deuteronomy 19:14-21, Hebrews 10:19-39

## Study Journal Question:

1. Why are we instructed to meet together?
2. What does Hebrews warn us about deliberate sin?
3. What is the importance of two or three witnesses?
4. What does it mean for you to live by faith?
5. How is God revealed in today's reading, and what does this mean for your life?

## Answers, Ponderings, and New Discoveries:

_____
_____
_____
_____
_____
_____
_____
_____
_____
_____
_____
_____
_____

**Prayer Requests / Answers :** _____
_____
_____
_____

## What is God doing around you, and how can you join Him?

_____
_____
_____

## Together Challenge:

Provoke other believers to love and good works.

      

## Daily Reading:

Psalm 102:1-28, Hebrews 11:1-22

## Study Journal Question:

1. How does the psalmist encouraged himself in the midst of trial?
2. How did the biblical examples help you define the meaning of faith?
3. Why do we need faith?
4. How has your faith been demonstrated?
5. How is God revealed in today's reading, and what does this mean for your life?

## Answers, Ponderings, and New Discoveries:

_____
_____
_____
_____
_____
_____
_____
_____
_____
_____
_____

**Prayer Requests / Answers :** _____
_____
_____
_____

## What is God doing around you, and how can you join Him?

_____
_____
_____

## Together Challenge:

Ask a believer how their faith has sustained them.

## Daily Reading:

Leviticus 21:1-22:16

## Study Journal Question:

1. Why was it important for the priest to remain clean?
2. What was required to go through the veil and enter God's holy presence?
3. What made the priests, the Tabernacle, and the sacrifices holy?
4. What does outward Holiness look like in your life?
5. How is God revealed in today's reading, and what does this mean for your life?

## Answers, Ponderings, and New Discoveries:

_____
_____
_____
_____
_____
_____
_____
_____
_____
_____
_____
_____

**Prayer Requests / Answers :** _____
_____
_____
_____

## What is God doing around you, and how can you join Him?

_____
_____
_____

## Together Challenge:

Show honor to someone in spiritual leadership.

## Daily Reading:

Leviticus 7:1-38

## Study Journal Question:

1. Why were Aaron and his sons given a portion of the offering?
2. What caused certain people to be cut off from among their nation?
3. What offerings were given for the priests to eat?
4. What do your sacrifices to the Lord look like?
5. How is God revealed in today's reading, and what does this mean for your life?

## Answers, Ponderings, and New Discoveries:

_____
_____
_____
_____
_____
_____
_____
_____
_____
_____
_____
_____

**Prayer Requests / Answers :** _____
_____
_____
_____

## What is God doing around you, and how can you join Him?

_____
_____
_____

## Together Challenge:

Invite friends over and give thanks to the Lord.

## Daily Reading:

Psalm 39:1-13, Leviticus 26:1-13, Hebrews 11:23-40

## Study Journal Question:

1. What things should we value in life considering how short it is?
2. What conditions did God give the Israelites to be blessed and mighty at war?
3. Why didn't the people in the Old Testament receive the things promised to them?
4. How have you walked by faith in your life?
5. How is God revealed in today's reading, and what does this mean for your life?

## Answers, Ponderings, and New Discoveries:

_____
_____
_____
_____
_____
_____
_____
_____
_____
_____
_____
_____

**Prayer Requests / Answers :** _____
_____
_____
_____

## What is God doing around you, and how can you join Him?

_____
_____
_____

## Together Challenge:

Remind someone to make the most of every opportunity because life is short.

## Daily Reading:
Proverbs 3:1-35, Hebrews 12:1-13

## Study Journal Question:

1. Why does God discipline His children?
2. How does Hebrews teach us to endure?
3. How valuable is wisdom?
4. What wisdom have you gained through God's discipline?
5. How is God revealed in today's reading, and what does this mean for your life?

## Answers, Ponderings, and New Discoveries:

_____
_____
_____
_____
_____
_____
_____
_____
_____
_____
_____
_____

**Prayer Requests / Answers :** _____
_____
_____
_____

## What is God doing around you, and how can you join Him?
_____
_____
_____

## Together Challenge:

Do not withhold good from whom it is due today.

## Daily Reading:

Leviticus 26:14-46, Hebrews 12:14-29

## Study Journal Question:

1. How does God respond to those who don't listen to him?
2. How do you strive for both peace and holiness in your relationships?
3. What did God warn the Israelites, and what does He warn us today?
4. Why is the New Covenant better than the Old Covenant?
5. How is God revealed in today's reading, and what does this mean for your life?

## Answers, Ponderings, and New Discoveries:

_____
_____
_____
_____
_____
_____
_____
_____
_____
_____
_____

**Prayer Requests / Answers :** _____
_____
_____
_____

## What is God doing around you, and how can you join Him?

_____
_____
_____

## Together Challenge:

In reverence and awe, worship God with others.

        

## Daily Reading:

Leviticus 4:1-35, Hebrews 13:1-25

## Study Journal Question:

1. How do the Old Testament sacrifices help us better understand what Jesus accomplished?
2. Why does God give us leaders?
3. How does knowing that God will never leave you or forsake you help you overcome fear?
4. What can we learn about God's perspective on unintentional sin, and what does this mean for us today?
5. How is God revealed in today's reading, and what does this mean for your life?

## Answers, Ponderings, and New Discoveries:

_____
_____
_____
_____
_____
_____
_____
_____
_____
_____
_____

**Prayer Requests / Answers :** _____
_____
_____
_____

## What is God doing around you, and how can you join Him?

_____
_____
_____

## Together Challenge:

Show hospitality to a stranger.

## Daily Reading:

Leviticus 11:1-47, Mark 5:1-20

## Study Journal Question:

1. Why did God give the Israelites clean and unclean laws?
2. Why would Jesus allow the unclean spirits to go into the unclean pigs?
3. Why were the people of the Gerasenes afraid?
4. Do you seek to be holy as God is holy?
5. How is God revealed in today's reading, and what does this mean for your life?

## Answers, Ponderings, and New Discoveries:

_____
_____
_____
_____
_____
_____
_____
_____
_____
_____
_____
_____

**Prayer Requests / Answers :** _____
_____
_____
_____

## What is God doing around you, and how can you join Him?

_____
_____
_____

## Together Challenge:

Go tell everyone how much Jesus has done for you.

# Daily Reading:

Leviticus 13:1-28

# Study Journal Question:

1. What was the role of the priest over the people of Israel?
2. What was the process to find out if someone had leprosy?
3. Why was it important for the people to know who had leprosy?
4. Who has God given you to help discern your spiritual condition?
5. How is God revealed in today's reading, and what does this mean for your life?

# Answers, Ponderings, and New Discoveries:

_____
_____
_____
_____
_____
_____
_____
_____
_____
_____
_____

**Prayer Requests / Answers :** _____
_____
_____
_____

# What is God doing around you, and how can you join Him?

_____
_____
_____

# Together Challenge:

Encourage someone with a chronic physical condition.

## Daily Reading:

Leviticus 13:29-59

## Study Journal Question:

1. How was a leprous person required to live?
2. What was required to be done to a leprous (or moldy) garment?
3. What judgment was the priest supposed to give concerning baldness?
4. How does leprosy represent a spiritual condition and how should you respond to it?
5. How is God revealed in today's reading, and what does this mean for your life?

## Answers, Ponderings, and New Discoveries:

_____
_____
_____
_____
_____
_____
_____
_____
_____
_____
_____

**Prayer Requests / Answers :** _____
_____
_____
_____

## What is God doing around you, and how can you join Him?

_____
_____
_____

## Together Challenge:

Recruit someone to help you remove what is destroying your spiritual life.

## Daily Reading:

Leviticus 14:1-32, Matthew 8:28-34

## Study Journal Question:

1. What was required of a leprous person to be cleansed?
2. How does God show compassion on the poor?
3. What did the demons understand about Jesus?
4. How have you seen Jesus' power over spiritual forces?
5. How is God revealed in today's reading, and what does this mean for your life?

## Answers, Ponderings, and New Discoveries:

_____
_____
_____
_____
_____
_____
_____
_____
_____
_____
_____
_____

**Prayer Requests / Answers :** _____
_____
_____
_____

## What is God doing around you, and how can you join Him?

_____
_____
_____

## Together Challenge:

Show compassion toward someone who is poor.

## Daily Reading:

Leviticus 14:33-57, Luke 8:26-39

## Study Journal Question:

1. How does leprosy in a house resemble sin in a person's life?
2. How does removing sin in your life resemble removing leprosy from a house?
3. Why did the demon identify himself as Legion?
4. How did the healed man respond to Jesus?
5. How is God revealed in today's reading, and what does this mean for your life?

## Answers, Ponderings, and New Discoveries:

_____
_____
_____
_____
_____
_____
_____
_____
_____
_____
_____
_____

**Prayer Requests / Answers :** _____
_____
_____

## What is God doing around you, and how can you join Him?

_____
_____
_____

## Together Challenge:

Ask someone to help make sure sin is not spreading in your life.

## Daily Reading:

Leviticus 15:1-33, Mark 5:21-43

## Study Journal Question:

1. How would you describe Jarius' faith?
2. How did Jesus demonstrate His power over unclean laws?
3. Is your faith more like Jarius or the people at his house? Why?
4. How did Jesus respond to the peoples' unbelief?
5. How is God revealed in today's reading, and what does this mean for your life?

## Answers, Ponderings, and New Discoveries:

_____
_____
_____
_____
_____
_____
_____
_____
_____
_____
_____
_____

**Prayer Requests / Answers :** _____
_____
_____
_____

## What is God doing around you, and how can you join Him?

_____
_____
_____

## Together Challenge:

Go to Jesus on behalf of someone else.

## Daily Reading:

Leviticus 17:1-16, Leviticus 24:1-9, Matthew 9:18-26

## Study Journal Question:

1. Why was God concerned about where a sacrifice was to be made?
2. What is the significance of a creature's blood?
3. Why did the woman touch Jesus?
4. What can you learn from the woman who touched Jesus?
5. How is God revealed in today's reading, and what does this mean for your life?

## Answers, Ponderings, and New Discoveries:

_____
_____
_____
_____
_____
_____
_____
_____
_____
_____
_____
_____

**Prayer Requests / Answers :** _____
_____
_____
_____

## What is God doing around you, and how can you join Him?

_____
_____
_____

## Together Challenge:

Provide some food to someone who ministers to you spiritually.

## Daily Reading:

Leviticus 24:10-25:7, Luke 8:40-56

## Study Journal Question:

1. What is the connection between faith and God's power?
2. If God's law about blasphemy were enforced today, how would it change our culture?
3. How did Jesus change the law concerning an eye for an eye and a tooth for a tooth?
4. How would the healed woman and Jairus respond to the trials in your life?
5. How is God revealed in today's reading, and what does this mean for your life?

## Answers, Ponderings, and New Discoveries:

_____
_____
_____
_____
_____
_____
_____
_____
_____
_____
_____

**Prayer Requests / Answers :** _____
_____
_____
_____

## What is God doing around you, and how can you join Him?

_____
_____
_____

## Together Challenge:

Share with someone about God's punishment for blasphemy and cursing.

## Daily Reading:

Leviticus 25:8-34

## Study Journal Question:

1. What was God's plan to prevent generational poverty?
2. How did the Levites differ from the rest of the Israelites in the Year of Jubilee?
3. How often was the Year of Jubilee?
4. How would you struggle if God commanded you not to make a living every 7 years?
5. How is God revealed in today's reading, and what does this mean for your life?

## Answers, Ponderings, and New Discoveries:

_____
_____
_____
_____
_____
_____
_____
_____
_____
_____
_____
_____

**Prayer Requests / Answers :** _____
_____
_____
_____

## What is God doing around you, and how can you join Him?

_____
_____
_____

## Together Challenge:

Help someone who is in poverty.

## Daily Reading:

Leviticus 27:1-34

## Study Journal Question:

1. What do people vow or dedicate to the Lord today?
2. What was required if someone wanted to redeem their gift to the Lord?
3. What types of vows did the Israelites give?
4. How does your giving reflect what's in your heart?
5. How is God revealed in today's reading, and what does this mean for your life?

## Answers, Ponderings, and New Discoveries:

_____
_____
_____
_____
_____
_____
_____
_____
_____
_____
_____

**Prayer Requests / Answers :** _____
_____
_____
_____

## What is God doing around you, and how can you join Him?

_____
_____
_____

## Together Challenge:

Honor God with a special gift.

## Daily Reading:

Leviticus 25:35-55, Matthew 9:27-34

## Study Journal Question:

1. What was the difference between an Israelite slave and a foreign slave?
2. How can you apply God's instructions about the poor to your life?
3. How did the blind men display their faith?
4. How do people deny Jesus today?
5. How is God revealed in today's reading, and what does this mean for your life?

## Answers, Ponderings, and New Discoveries:

_____
_____
_____
_____
_____
_____
_____
_____
_____
_____
_____
_____

**Prayer Requests / Answers :** _____
_____
_____
_____

## What is God doing around you, and how can you join Him?

_____
_____
_____

## Together Challenge:

Talk to someone about what it means to have faith.

## Daily Reading:

Numbers 2:1-34, Matthew 10:1-15

## Study Journal Question:

1. How did the 12 become able to work miracles?
2. What is the significance of describing the 12 as both apostles and disciples?
3. Where did Jesus send the twelve?
4. How would you respond if Jesus called you to go on a journey without provisions?
5. How is God revealed in today's reading, and what does this mean for your life?

## Answers, Ponderings, and New Discoveries:

_____
_____
_____
_____
_____
_____
_____
_____
_____
_____
_____
_____

**Prayer Requests / Answers :** _____
_____
_____
_____

## What is God doing around you, and how can you join Him?

_____
_____
_____

## Together Challenge:

Draw the Israelite encampment around the Tabernacle based on the size of each tribe and show it to a friend.

## Daily Reading:

Numbers 3:1-32, Matthew 10:16-42

## Study Journal Question:

1. What is the job of the Kohathites?
2. How does Jesus command us to fear differently from those in the world?
3. Who will Jesus acknowledge before the Father?
4. How can you find your life by losing it?
5. How is God revealed in today's reading, and what does this mean for your life?

## Answers, Ponderings, and New Discoveries:

_____
_____
_____
_____
_____
_____
_____
_____
_____
_____
_____
_____

**Prayer Requests / Answers :** _____
_____
_____
_____

## What is God doing around you, and how can you join Him?

_____
_____
_____

## Together Challenge:

Do something kind for a disciple of Jesus.

## Daily Reading:

Numbers 3:33-51, Numbers 4:34-49

## Study Journal Question:

1. How old were the people who served in the tent of meeting?
2. How did God redeem the firstborn of Israel?
3. Where did Moses and Aaron camp? Why?
4. What do you do in service toward the Lord?
5. How is God revealed in today's reading, and what does this mean for your life?

## Answers, Ponderings, and New Discoveries:

_____
_____
_____
_____
_____
_____
_____
_____
_____
_____
_____

**Prayer Requests / Answers :** _____
_____
_____
_____

## What is God doing around you, and how can you join Him?

_____
_____
_____

## Together Challenge:

Serve the people in your church.